Synergistic Evangelism

Dr. Darrell W. Robinson

CROSS
BOOKS

CrossBooks™
1663 Liberty Drive
Bloomington, IN 47403
www.crossbooks.com
Phone: 1-866-879-0502

First published by CrossBooks 6/2/2009

ISBN: 978-1-6150-7004-6 (sc)

Printed in the United States of America
Bloomington, Indiana

This book is printed on acid-free paper.

Contents

FOREWORD FOR:

Darrell Robinson, *Synergistic Evangelism*

Darrell Robinson has birthed a book filled with life and passion in his *Synergistic Evangelism*. It comes at a needy time for all New Testament churches. While many North American churches are dying for lack of evangelistic fervor, Darrell calls the church back to its first love.

In *Synergistic Evangelism,* Dr. Robinson combines the experience of a veteran pastor, the gentleness of a personal soul winner, and the fire of a God-called evangelist. Darrell's passion for reaching the lost and love for the church jump off every page. As a matter of fact, this book is truly unique in its field. It clearly explains transferable methods for evangelism that every church can and should be using. It is thorough, without being overwhelming, very practical, and a good read.

I am often humbled by the natural and gracious way that Darrell shares the Gospel. In the pages of *Synergistic Evangelism*, Robinson gives narrations of time-tested and proven ways to share the Gospel: the Roman Road, John 3, the Lifeline, and Beautiful Baptism. These methods are biblically and theologically sound, and they lead lost souls to look at the crucified Savior. I have heard Darrell draw persons into Gospel presentations. He is genuine and winsome without downgrading sin or the cross. And God's Spirit uses him mightily.

This book is a must for pastors and students of evangelism. It effectively combines personal evangelism with church evangelism. I plan to use it in all my Basic Evangelism classes.

Darrell is a great encouragement to me. He is definitely a man that practices what he preaches! Because it is biblical and by the grace of God, there is hope for the future of local church evangelism if we would only take to heart the teaching in *Synergistic Evangelism*.

Thomas P. Johnston, Ph.D.
Associate Professor of Evangelism,
Midwestern Baptist Theological Seminary.

INTRODUCTION

The book of Acts records Jesus' strategy for reaching the world with the Gospel. Acts describes five techniques that were used by the first century church in reaching the lost for Christ. When a church implements all five of these techniques in reaching the lost of its community, they will be synergistic in producing a great harvest of souls.

A word study of "synergism" is profitable for us in growing evangelistic churches. The definition of synergism in the Merriam-Webster Online Dictionary is: "Synergism, in general, may be defined as two or more agents working together to produce a result not obtainable by any of the agents independently. The word synergy or synergism comes from two Greek words: *erg* meaning "to work," and *syn* meaning "together," hence synergism is a "working together."

Merriam-Webster goes on to say, "Synergism is the interaction of conditions such that the total effect is greater than the sum of the individual effects."

Synergism is observable in Acts. The New Testament churches practiced the strategy of Jesus, reflected by Paul's statement to the Corinthians, "I have become all things to all people, so that I may by all means save some" (1 Corinthians 9:22b HCSB). The five techniques, or means, are synergistic. They are: public proclamation, caring ministry, event attraction, geographic saturation, and personal presentation of the gospel. When local churches incorporate all five in their evangelistic strategy, the interaction of all five will be synergistic.

CHAPTER ONE
Jesus' Strategy for Reaching Our World

He was alive! Jesus had risen from the dead! For forty days he met with his followers and by many infallible proofs showed himself to be alive. He gave commands and instructions. Then, just before ascending back to the Father, he met with his disciples for one last time before ascending. He gave them his one last word. Last words are words of critical importance, words of mission, and words of vision.

"But you will receive power when the Holy Spirit has come upon you, you will be My witnesses in Jerusalem, in all Judea and Samaria, and to the ends of the earth" (Acts 1:8 HCSB). Jesus spoke these words to his disciples. While they watched, he began to rise from them. The cloud of God's Shekinah glory received him out of their sight.

Two angels stood by them and spoke. "Men of Galilee, why are you standing here gazing?" I would have been gazing too! What a sight! Nothing like this had ever happened. Jesus had ascended to the Father. The angels continued, "This same Jesus, who was taken up from you into heaven, will so come in like manner as you saw him go into heaven."

It was as if the angels were saying, "Jesus is coming again! Now, get about what he told you to do. They went back into Jerusalem into an upper room and continued for ten days in extraordinary praying. They

1

needed it! They had just received an impossible mission from their Lord—to take the Gospel of Christ's death, burial, and resurrection to every person in their world and to call them to repentance and faith in him. Impossible! They were so few! So ordinary were they. So shallow were they in their understanding of him and his mission. On their way up the road from Jericho to Jerusalem where he would be crucified, Jesus was communicating that he was about to go to the cross. But the apostles did not hear because they were so preoccupied by their own agendas. They were jostling one another and competing about who would sit on his right hand and who would sit on his left hand. They did not comprehend the heart of Jesus! Religious politics and position seeking today is degrading and minimizing the true work of the kingdom of God!

They needed and we need extraordinary prayer that will bring us to intimacy with God, brokenness, repentance, and yielding to God! When this happened as the day of Pentecost arrived, they were "all in one place *in one accord.*" In one accord are three English words translating one Greek word, "homothumodon" (Acts 1:14 and Acts 2:1). The word was used in reference to the smoldering embers on the altar of incense in the temple. It means "having the same fire." When the disciples reached brokenness, repentance, and yielding to God through extraordinary prayer, they came to have the same fire—the same passion. The passion is a Jesus passion, a passion for the souls of the lost. This is true unity. It brought them together so that they did not think of themselves and their agendas—only Jesus and his mission. They came to obedience to Jesus and his mandate in Acts 1:8 to witness. This is revival!

At that moment "there came a sound from heaven as of a rushing mighty wind." Divine of energy! Divided tongues of fire rested on each of them and they began to speak in other languages. Divine expression! They spoke the Gospel to people in the languages of the many nations from which they had come.

When the disciples of Jesus came to brokenness, repentance, and yielding to God, they came to have "the same fire," and obedience to Christ's mission. God miraculously broke down the barriers for them to communicate the Gospel to all nations. Peter stood up and preached Christ. He gave a clear invitation for them to repent and be baptized, committing themselves to the Christ who had just been crucified, but rose again. About three thousand people gladly received the Word and were baptized that same day.

Today, when the people of a church come to brokenness, repentance, and yielding to God, they come to have the same fire and passion, and they are obedient to Christ's mission to reach every person with the Gospel. God will break down whatever barrier there may be for them to reach the lost for Christ. A church can experience revival and reach the lost! His priority must be our priority!

Culture

One of the present-day excuses for churches not intentionally witnessing to the lost is that "our culture today has changed. They do not want to hear the Gospel." This is a *myth*, a cop-out! A myth is something we think is true, but is really not true. If we think it is true, we begin to act as if it is true. Then it becomes true to us! Satan, then, has us where he wants us—paralyzed regarding evangelism. There are numerous "myths" that Satan has peddled in churches regarding evangelism.

The reality is our culture has changed and is changing. Cultures are always changing, but the Bible and Jesus' strategy for reaching the lost never changes. People's spiritual needs are always the same. Our culture is reverting toward the culture of the first century when Christ was hated and Christianity was under attack. This did not change the mission of believers in the first century. They were committed to take the Gospel to every person. Their power was the Holy Spirit and the Gospel of Christ (Romans 1:16 HCSB). "For I am not ashamed of the Gospel, because it is the God's power for salvation to everyone who believes, first to the Jew, and also to the Greek."

Believers *will* be committed to Christ and his mission to witness faithfully to the lost. If pastors and leaders buy into the myth that they do not want to witness, then they lower their expectation for the level of commitment for which Christ calls. The result is the level of the people's performance and obedience to witness is lowered.

In Angola, Africa, I was leading a conference for one hundred pastors who had come in from the different provinces at great difficulty. They traveled in any way they could by foot, bicycle, bus, and boat. At the conference they slept on concrete or dirt floors. They ate raw

3

manioc to sustain themselves. We met from 8:00 AM to 6:00 PM with no night meetings because of the danger. All day they participated in the Conference on Reaching Angola for Christ with enthusiasm.

I was speaking on commitment. The Holy Spirit brought me under conviction. I said, "I have no right to speak to you about commitment after all you have been through. You have told me that from 1965 to 1972 you were in civil war. Then, the Communists took over and until 2002 you underwent severe persecution. In 2002, the Communist system fell and your country and you are now rebuilding your decimated infrastructure. You tell me about commitment.

A pastor stood and reported, "Nine of our pastors and evangelists were arrested by the Communists. They were locked in a building. The Communists set fire to it and burned them alive because they would not renounce Jesus!"

Another shared, "Our convention president, Mario Vontade, was a bi-vocational pastor and school teacher. He was arrested and told that he could not be a pastor and a teacher. They said he would poison the minds of the students. The captain put a pistol to Mario's head and shouted to him, 'Renounce Jesus or I will kill you!' Mario responded, 'I will not renounce Jesus! He is my life!'"

The captain threw him to the floor and ordered a company of seventy-five soldiers to stomp the life out of him. They stomped and stomped to cave in his chest. Mario was bleeding at the mouth. They left him for dead. But, miraculously, God raised him up and Mario became a great leader of Angola Baptists.

Believers will, indeed, be committed to Christ and his mission. One of the men remarked, "We view Christianity in America as a Disneyworld religion where church people simply want to come and be entertained."

We must not lower the level of Jesus' expectations for commitment. "If anyone desires to come after me, let him deny himself, and take up the cross, and follow me" (Matthew 16:24 NKJV).

The power of God for salvation is not in our cleverness, not in our religious entertainment, not in our slick advertisements or programs, not in avoiding biblical truth to keep from offending people. The power is in the Gospel of Christ. But, some have lost confidence in the power of the Gospel!

We are told that people today do not want Christians to come to see them or approach them with the Gospel. How do they know this? Their answer is that they have surveyed the non-churched and come to this conclusion. The truth is that this, too, is a myth and a cop-out! If the early Christians had believed and behaved like this, the Gospel would not have survived the first century. They prayed that God would give them boldness to share Jesus no matter what they did to them (Acts 4:29-31).

In the first place, we do not go because they want us to come, but because he has sent us. Second, lost people do not know what it will take for them to reach Christ. When I was lost, if you had asked me, "Do you want a Christian to come to your house and talk to you?" I would have strongly said, "Absolutely NOT!" But that is exactly what I needed and that is what happened for me to be saved. They came to see me.

If you ask lost people what it will take to reach them for Christ, you are asking the wrong people. They do not know what it will take to reach them for Christ. They are spiritually blind and need the light of the Gospel to open their understanding as to where they are and how they need Christ.

Jesus' Plan—Acts 1:8

"But you will receive power when the Holy Spirit has come upon you, and you will be My witnesses in Jerusalem, in all Judea and Samaria, and to the ends of the earth"(Acts 1:8 HCSB).

In Acts 1:8 Jesus gave us his concentrated plan to reach the world with the Gospel:

The Power: The Holy Spirit! Holy Spirit power is adequate! He can get the job done! Holy Spirit power is available! He lives in you if you are saved. He will work through you as you share the Gospel of Christ.

The Priority: Witness for Christ! This is the priority of every pastor, church leader, and church member.

The Personnel: "You" includes every Christian. Witnessing is every Christian's job! When every Christian is faithful to Christ in witness, multitudes will be reached for Christ.

The Plan: "In Jerusalem, Judea, Samaria, and to the ends of the earth." Every local church begins with their Jerusalem (primary ministry area), and saturates their Jerusalem with the Gospel-sharing. They continue to reach out until they are reaching people for Christ to the ends of the earth.

Jesus' strategy to reach our world is centered on the local church. Acts 1:8 is Jesus' strategy of each local church to practice total evangelism—to intentionally share Christ with every person in such a way that each person can respond with understanding to the claims of Christ on his or her life. To implement total evangelism requires the church to practice total penetration of its Jerusalem (primary ministry area) with the Gospel through total participation of the membership in evangelistic witness to the lost. His strategy will be fulfilled as each local church consistently implements total evangelism. The five evangelistic techniques in the book of acts is the key to implementing total evangelism.

Paul's ministry in Ephesus is a biblical example in Acts 19:10. Within two years, every person in Asia received the Gospel through the evangelistic witness of the church of Ephesus. Paul, as far as we know, did not leave the city of Ephesus. He did what Jesus said to do. He reached people for Christ, equipped them to reach others, and they saturated Asia with the Gospel of Christ.

In every church where I was pastor, we practiced Jesus' strategy to reach our Jerusalem. Every church grew significantly and we baptized many. Today I am assisting churches to follow Jesus' strategy. It is still working. Jesus' strategy worked then and it works now!

CHAPTER TWO
The First Evangelistic Message

When the Holy Spirit came and filled the church with power, all the disciples shared the Gospel personally with people from many nations (Acts 2). Then Peter stood and preached the great Christ-centered message of Pentecost. The disciples had been accused of being drunk because they were miraculously sharing the Gospel in languages they had not known. Peter told them that the disciples were not drunk at all, but that this was the fulfillment of the prophesy of Joel, the prophet. Then he preached Christ! He charged them with the sin of crucifying Christ, the Son of God. Peter preached the truth, risking the alienation of the hearers. Boldly, he preached the truth in love. He did not minimize the truth out of fear that he would offend them.

Peter declared the resurrection of Jesus Christ by the power of God and showed that it was prophesied by David in Old Testament scriptures. He told them that Christ has been seated at the right hand of God. He continued by saying that now God has poured out his Holy Spirit who is responsible for the things they are seeing and hearing which was predicted by the prophet.

At that point the convicted crowd "when they heard this, they were cut to the heart, and said to Peter and the rest of the apostles, 'Brothers, what must we do?'" (Acts 2:37 HCSB).

Simon Peter, who had cowardly denied his Lord, courageously told them what they must do! He extended the first public invitation of the New Testament Church. It was natural, logical, and the biblical conclusion of the Spirit-filled message.

Invitation

It is biblical and logical that an invitation for hearers to respond and receive Christ should follow a presentation of the Gospel.

Peter's response was an invitation for them to publicly commit their lives to Christ. "Repent," Peter said to them, "and be baptized, each of you, in the name of Jesus the Messiah for the forgiveness of your sins, and you will receive the gift of the Holy Spirit" (Acts 2:38 HCSB).

The first Christian sermon was one in which Peter explained the death, burial, and resurrection of Christ. He confronted the hearers with their sin. He called on them to repent of their sin and be baptized in the name of the one who was crucified. Their baptism was their outward confession of faith in the risen Lord Jesus.

Baptism

Baptism was their first step of obedience and identification with Christ as Savior and Lord. We must remember that Jesus had just been crucified. His followers had been persecuted and even jailed. Christianity was illegal and unacceptable to the culture. Their baptism meant that they were identifying their lives as followers of the one who had just been crucified.

Why be baptized? Today, baptism means less to many than it did in the first century. To be baptized today means for many that one identifies with the church. It is socially acceptable. In the first century people were identifying themselves as followers of the one who had just been crucified. It meant that they faced rejection by society. Their family might turn against them. They could suffer social rejection of the community. They could be economically boycotted and people might refuse to do business with them or they might be fired from their jobs. They might even be killed. Some followers of Christ were drowned after their baptism. They were held under the water and told, "You like water, get all you want of it." They were drowned.

Baptism does two things. First, it testifies to an event. It also testifies to an experience. Baptism symbolizes or pictures the event of Christ's death, burial, and resurrection. When the new believer stands in the water, the water crosses the body. This forms a cross. The new believer is testifying that he or she believes that Jesus died on the cross to provide forgiveness for his or her sin. As the believer is lowered under the water, it symbolizes their belief that Christ was buried in a tomb. As the body of the believer is raised up, it symbolizes the resurrection of Jesus.

Through baptism, a believer says, "I believe that Christ died for my sins, that he was buried, and that he rose from the dead! He lives today! I have received him and he lives in my heart and life. No matter what others may do, you will find me following Jesus. I am committed to obey him."

Baptism symbolizes an experience. As the believer stands in the water, it symbolizes the spiritually dead person without Christ. What do we do with dead people? We bury them. As the believer is lowered in the water, it symbolizes the death of the old life of sin and the burial of the old life identifying with Jesus' death and burial. As the believer is raised up, it symbolizes that Christ has entered the Believer's life and raised him or her up to live a new life following Christ.

Baptism is beautiful expression of what Jesus did for us and has done in us.

Does baptism save? Is baptism essential to salvation? The answer is, "No!" Salvation is by grace through faith in Jesus Christ and not by works (Ephesians 2:8). But, a saved person will want to obey Jesus and be baptized!

Personally, when I was thirteen years of age, I wanted to be saved, but I had procrastinated because I was afraid to be baptized. I was afraid of water. Having grown up in West Texas where it seldom rains and water is never more than knee-deep, I had not learned to swim. I used to wish that if my family did go to church, they would go to the Methodist Church instead of the Baptist Church so I could get sprinkled, not dunked in the water. I was afraid that the pastor might drown me.

My mother and father, Lillie and Woner Robinson, spoke to me about my being saved one night following our attendance of a revival service at Salem Baptist Church. The next morning, my dad prayed with me and I received Christ. We went to the revival services and though terrified, I confessed Christ. On Sunday night I was baptized. I was scared, but I had received Jesus as my Savior and Lord. I wanted to obey his command to be baptized. I would have done it if the pastor had drowned me. Christ changed my life!

Discipleship

In Acts 2:39-42 HCSB those who were baptized, "devoted themselves to the apostles' teaching, to fellowship, to the breaking of bread, and to prayers."

The New Testament church evangelized and led people to Christ, and discipled them. Their method was that they involved them by leading them to continue under the apostles' teaching. The church must teach new believers biblical basics and how to live their daily lives following Christ. They need to be taught how to live a victorious life daily, how to study their Bible daily, how to pray, how to practice biblical stewardship beginning with tithing, and how to witness and lead those who need him to Christ.

When I received Christ and followed him in baptism, I did all I know to do. I started attending church services, but no one told me anything about how to grow in Christ. After a while, I began to drift spiritually. When you drift, you do not drift toward Christ and Christian living. You drift away! And that is what I did until a pastor came into my life who took an interest in me. He gradually began to spend time with me. Without my knowing it, he was discipling me.

Here is how the pastor got me involved. It was humorous. The first religious thing I did was haul off the pastor's trash. We lived in a small town where there was no garbage collection. Every family took care of their own trash. We burned our trash in fifty-five gallon barrels behind the house. When the barrels were full, it was my job to load them in the pick-up truck and haul them to the dump. Our pastor, Mark Reeves, saw what I did. He asked me to stop by his house and haul off his trash when I took ours to the dump. I was glad to do it. Pastor Mark would always help me load it and sometimes he went with me. He spent time with me and shared with me. What was he doing and why? Of course, he wanted to get rid of his trash! But, he had more in mind than that.

He wanted to get to know me and disciple me. He saw something in me that God could use, though I was not really religious.

Eventually, God called me to preach. As a pastor, I determined that I would try not to allow those we reached for Christ duplicate my experience of drifting in spiritual ignorance. I prepared material to train my congregation and I spent time teaching them how to grow in Christ. Many pastors and churches are using the little booklet I prepared titled "What's Next?" with the subtitle "Grow in Christ." It has seven chapters on the basics of how to grow in Christ.

The new believers need to be incorporated into the fellowship of the church. They should participate in a small group Bible study such as a Sunday school class. The class should minister and include the new believer in fellowship, service, and outreach. The class will provide accountability, which is needed by every person. A class member should be assigned to the new member as a sponsor and encourager to mentor him or her.

Dr. Waylon Moore, a great soulwinner and discipler, in his May 2008 issue of mentoring says, "We begin the Christian life as a spiritual baby. A baby needs four things constantly to grow strong into maturity: loving, feeding, protection, and training ... every believer needs a mentor with a parent heart to carry them if need be or help them up when they fall. We need volunteers trained to adopt those new babes. They need prayer immediately, and then help to begin growing that same week."

New members need to be assimilated immediately into the life of the church. If new members are not assimilated into the fellowship of the church, form positive relationships, join ministry and witness, they will eventually drop out or leave and go to another church.

The pattern of the New Testament church was to involve every member in ministry and witness. That is the way the church moved from addition of disciples (Acts 2:41) to multiplication of disciples (Acts 6:7). Every member was involved in the mission of Christ to reach the lost with the Gospel. Those who were reached were immediately involved in sharing Jesus with others.

The best method to disciple new believers is to involve them as quickly as possible in witnessing for Christ to their family, friends, acquaintances, and the people they meet for Christ. Witnessing drives the believer to Bible study to know how to "tell the story of Jesus."

Witnessing drives the believer to prayer. Leading people to Christ is a Holy Spirit work. Prayer involves us with the Holy Spirit in his power in reaching the lost. Witnessing drives the believer to deal with his or her wrong habits. Inconsistent living diffuses the power to effectively share the Gospel. It negates the witness of the believer. As believers yield to the Holy Spirit, his power flows through obedient witness for Jesus.

Local churches need to develop a definite plan to follow up and disciple new believers. Each should be assigned to an individual who will be an encourager and a mentor. A Sunday School class or Bible Study group should take the responsibility to enlist them in Bible study, incorporate them into the fellowship of the Body of Christ, and engage them in service and witness for Christ.

CHAPTER THREE
Public Proclamation

Five techniques are found in the book of Acts through which the New Testament Church reached the lost for Christ. They are: public proclamation, caring ministry, event attraction, geographic saturation, and personal presentation of the Gospel. The five are *synergistic*. (The word means that they work together for an enhanced effect.)

The first of the five techniques in the book of Acts for reaching the lost is public proclamation. Public proclamation is the preaching and teaching of the Gospel publicly. Every church engages in public proclamation. But, the question is—is what we are doing effectively evangelistic? For it to be effective in reaching the lost for Christ, the lost must be in the church where the Gospel is being preached or taught. Or the church has to take the proclamation out to the lost.

Almost every church engages in proclamation, but much of it is not evangelistic, and does not reach the lost for Christ. Most preaching is made up of interesting homilies and excellent oratory, but does not present the Gospel of Christ and call people to Christ.

If our proclamation is to be evangelistic, it will have these characteristics. It will be preaching anointed by the Holy Spirit. The preacher will preach the truth with passion for Christ and for the lost. The Gospel will be shared in a clear and easy to understand manner with the plan of salvation explained carefully. Then, the invitation for the lost to receive Christ will be extended. The lost will be called to repent, receive Christ, and confess him as Savior and Lord. Peter is our biblical example in Acts 2.

Teaching is a second-way proclamation can be used to lead the lost to Christ. In Sunday school classes, Bible studies, and home or cell groups, the Gospel can be shared and an invitation for people to pray and receive Christ can be extended. When people receive Christ, they need to be guided by someone in the group. The basics of the steps to take as a new believer should be covered with them.

Worship Services that are Evangelistic

How can a church be effective in developing worship services that are distinctly evangelistic? Every worship service should accomplish three priorities: glorify God and praise the Lord Jesus; train and equip believers through the preaching of the Bible; and present the Gospel and reach the lost for Christ. What elements in a worship service can make the difference in making every service a harvest time for souls?

First, it can happen as the church develops a *climate* of evangelistic concern and urgency. To develop such a climate is an ongoing process. Members need to be equipped to share the Gospel and be involved in seeking to reach them for Christ. Much emphasis needs to be given to what it means to be lost. Members will develop a passion for reaching the lost.

A church with a climate of evangelistic concern and urgency will welcome guests who attend with genuine care and interest. It is easy to be superficial in welcoming people we meet in church. They need to have people reach out to them, get acquainted, and, perhaps, even invite them to lunch or for refreshments. Such a climate causes members to see others as God sees them—as treasures to God who have unlimited potential. When we meet guests at a church service we should get their names, remember them, and call their names the next time they come. Secure their address if possible. Write their names and addresses in your address book so you can follow up. Then, give their names and addresses to the pastor or evangelism leader for follow up.

A fine young pastor of a rural church where new people were moving in to work in plants along the river developed an emphasis that he called "Priority Five." Priority Five meant that he asked every member to spend the first five minutes after they arrived at the church facility looking for someone they did not know. They were instructed to go to the person and get acquainted. They were to welcome them and begin a friendship. The person may be a guest or a member that they do not know well. Then, after "Priority Five," they move on to visit with their usual friends and close associates. In spite of its location, the church was reaching people and growing dynamically.

Second, develop a spirit of celebrative worship and praise. Involve the people in singing and praising our Lord. Evangelistic soloists, singing groups, and choirs are effective in growing such a spirit. Heartfelt singing honors our Lord and lifts us nearer to him spiritually. Paul associates being filled with the Holy Spirit with an expression of "speaking to one another in psalms, hymns and spiritual songs, singing and making music to the Lord in your heart" (Ephesians 5:18-19 HCSB). What makes the singing, music, and praise meaningful? Not style, but spirit and substance. Many styles of music are effectively used to worship our Lord and evangelize the lost. God uses various means to move the human heart and soul toward Him. One of the most meaningful times of worship that I have experienced was in an early morning worship service in New Jersey. In the service the leader used quiet music and silence. The silence ministered greatly to my heart, allowing me to commune with God with no distraction. God uses silence to glorify himself. "But the Lord is in His holy temple; let everyone on earth be silent in His presence" (Habakkuk 2:20 HCSB).

God uses hymns, spiritual songs, singing, and melodious instruments to make melody to the Lord. "Praise Him with trumpet blast; praise Him with harp and lyre. Praise Him with tambourine and dance; praise Him with flute and strings. Praise Him with resounding cymbals; praise Him with clashing cymbals. Let everything that breathes praise the Lord. Hallelujah" (Psalm 150:3-5 HCSB)! God desires our praise to his glory! It is quite a shame that we condemn and reject one another because one desires to praise him in "hymns" and another in "spiritual songs." Why don't we decide to praise him in the unity of his Spirit, accept one another for his glory, and reach the lost for Christ?

The people involved in music and singing can do much to create a climate for evangelism. Each should be a consistent witness for Christ, seeking to lead someone to Christ. At First Baptist Church in Odessa, Texas, the minister of music, Curtis Brewer, led the choir to participate in witness training. He challenged every member to commit to seek to reach at one lost person for Christ and the church within the year. All of them did so. They named one hundred lost people they were seeking to reach. What a difference it made both in the lives of choir members and in the worship services.

When a choir member saw a person for whom they were praying and were attempting to reach come into the congregation, he or she was filled with joy and prayed through the entire service for that person. Such a joyful and prayerful spirit will spread through the congregation and do much to lift the spirit of the worship service.

Third, prayer is an essential element of a great evangelistic worship service. It is good to have an opportunity for worshippers to participate in prayer. Some churches invite people who desire to come forward and kneel for prayer while soft, worshipful music plays. Others have pastors, deacons, and church leaders to stand at the front to meet the people and pray with them if they desire. People who have a prayer need are invited to come forward to pray with one of them or to pray privately.

As a pastor, I invited the people who desired to come for prayer to do so. Among others, a couple came forward and knelt. They were newcomers to our community whom I had visited the previous week. They said that they were from a Catholic background. I had given them the directions to the nearest Catholic church, but invited them to visit us if they had an opportunity. As they knelt for prayer, they appeared concerned. I spoke to them and they responded. Both desired to know Christ. I prayed with them and they accepted Christ. They said that they were accustomed to kneeling for prayer when they went to the Catholic churches, but they did not know Christ. They were baptized and became faithful members of our church. Prayer opens the hearts of people to Christ.

It is good for the pastor and church staff to lead in prayer in worship services. But it is also healthy for various members of different age-groups to offer public prayers. This involves the people. It says to the congregation that all of us can pray. I have visited churches where only the pastor prayed. He prayed the pastoral prayer, the offertory prayer, the closing prayer. This left the impression that only the pastor is qualified to pray. We want to communicate in word and actions that God's heart is open to the prayers of all of our people.

Fourth, the testimonies of God's people reach the hearts of others and are a strengthening force in an evangelistic service. People are captivated by human interest stories, especially spiritual human interest stories. God works mightily as his people share what God has been doing in their lives. As a pastor, I incorporated what I called "report and share time" in our services. I taught our people how to share a one-minute testimony. During a worship service, I would state that we are about to have a three minute "report and share time," then ask two or three who are led of God to report and share about what God had been doing in and through their lives and witness this week to come forward to the front row. I would step down from the platform with a microphone and conduct about a one-minute interview as one of them reported. I would always hold the microphone. Do not ever hand them the microphone. People often do not know how to quit. Always God moved. It accomplished two purposes. First, our people heard them with empathy and interest. It was an example of what God can do through the average Christian. Second, it enhanced the spirit of evangelism in the church. I made a point of asking them to share what God did through their witness for Christ. Sometimes they shared about an attempt to witness when the person refused to permit them to do it. It was real and not always a success story. That gave me the opportunity to help our people understand that "God did not call us to success, but to faithfulness." God uses our witness to sometimes "sow the seed of the Gospel" and sometimes to "harvest" as people receive Christ.

In one particular service one of the older deacons said, "Thank you, pastor, for your emphasis on witnessing and for equipping us to witness. I have served in the Deacon Hospital Ministry. Every week, I go to the hospital and visit room-to-room and have prayer with patients. My problem is I have left my first love. Since our witness training and emphasis, I have gone down the halls witnessing. This week I led three people to Christ. I got back to my first work. Now, my first love is back." What a testimony! God used that one-minute testimony in a greater way than the sermon that day.

People sharing witnessing testimonies will say to the congregation, "That person was used of God. Maybe God can use me, too." This contributes to creating the climate of evangelistic concern.

Fifth, God-anointed preaching of the Gospel is an essential element of true worship. Often, the impression is left that music and singing is worship. The person in charge of leading music is often called "worship minister or worship pastor." This betrays a lack of biblical understanding in churches. Some leave the impression that only music and singing are worship. Worship is more than music and singing. Major parts of worship are prayer, testimony, and God-anointed preaching as well as music and singing. Many elements are present to create true worship. The preaching of the Word in the power of the Holy Spirit is central. God-anointed preaching is essential. Not every preacher can speak homiletically and with oratorical genius, but any preacher who spends time in the study of the Word and intense prayer can be a Spirit-filled and God-anointed preacher of the Gospel.

My pastor was not a good speaker. One had to listen intently to get his message. While his delivery was lacking, the content of his sermon was biblical, soundly doctrinal, and evangelistic. Revival broke out in the church and community because of his preaching. He studied the Word! He prayed and sought God's direction and anointing. He preached God's Word with the anointing and power of God. Then he moved the message to a climax with a warm and loving evangelistic invitation. God works mightily when his Word is preached in the power of the Holy Spirit.

The power to change the lives of people is through the preaching of the Word! "For Christ did not send me to baptize, but to preach the gospel—not with clever words, so that the cross of Christ will not be emptied of its effect. For to those who are perishing the message of the cross is foolishness, but to us who are being saved it is God's power" (1 Corinthians 1:17-18 HCSB).

Sixth, an evangelistic invitation appeal for the lost to receive and commit their lives to Christ and for Christians to experience a renewal of their commitment to Him is a natural conclusion for a biblical and meaningful worship service. In such a spiritual climate of commitment to Christ's commission the lost will be reached through public proclamation!

The other four evangelistic techniques are essential if public proclamation is to be as effective as it can be. If a church engages in caring ministry, event attraction, geographic saturation, and personal presentation, it will be synergistic. Many more will come for the public proclamation and the harvest can be multiplied! An evangelistic invitation is paramount if the lost are to come to Christ.

How to Give an Evangelistic Invitation

Through the years many of our pastors in churches large and small effectively preach God-anointed Gospel messages and extend an evangelistic invitation. Lost people have received and confessed Christ and believers have been renewed and revived. These churches have grown and are growing. These pastors and churches believe that the entire worship service points toward the invitation for people to personally experience Christ. I heard Billy Graham say that he always began the invitation in his sermon introduction.

However, there is a growing trend among pastors to minimize the importance of the invitation. Some have completely stopped conducting a public evangelistic invitation. Others simply explain that an interested person can meet the pastor following the service or contact the church office for an appointment. Still others ask that an interested person check on the card or worship guide that they desire to make a decision and want a pastoral visit.

What are the reasons for such attitudes toward the public invitation? The reasons are varied. First, many pastors preach great sermons and simply say, "Now we will have the invitation. If you want to come, then, come." There is no explanation of the Gospel and what to do! How tragic! The people do not know what to do. Therefore, the invitation is simply an add-on and is not effective. Rather than learning how to effectively extend the invitation, some drop it altogether.

Second, church style influences attitudes. Some "seeker sensitive" pastors do not want to offend by putting people on the spot. Some have moved away from the public invitation altogether.

Third, theological perspective has caused some to depart from the practice of extending an invitation. Their strong emphasis on the sovereignty of God has led some to view a public invitation as a work of man rather than the work of God. This seems to be the attitude faced by the first Baptist missionary to India, William Carey. He was told, "If God wants the heathen saved, he can save them without us."

I encountered this attitude when I preached an evangelistic mission in Scotland. A deacon was offended when I extended an invitation. He was also offended when I encouraged people to witness to others and make an effort to lead them to Christ. He said, "No! We do not talk to people about their decision for Christ. That is God's work. If we do it, we may get people that God does not want!"

Fourth, some have stopped having an invitation because the pastor does not know how. He feels the pressure and fear of failure if no one comes forward. The solution could be to study the invitation and how to extend it. He could seek the Holy Spirit's anointing and trust him to work in the invitation.

In reality, the invitation is the work of God. He does use the preacher to preach the Word and call people to come to Christ. It is the Holy Spirit who uses the Word as his sword to pierce hearts and minds with conviction and draw them to Christ. Paul testified, "Knowing, then the fear of the Lord, we persuade people" (2 Corinthians 5:11 HCSB).

Suggestions for extending an evangelistic invitation:

Pray for the service, for the invitation, for the lost, and for God's anointing and passion in your own life.

Plan for the invitation. The entire service should point to and prepare for the invitation. The music, the sermon, and everything in the service should guide hearers to be ready to respond to Christ at the time of invitation. Decide on the alternate approaches you can take as the Holy Spirit leads during the invitation. Plan for the wording you will use with each alternate approach.

Be sure to have prepared counselors available at the front to assist as people come forward and take the pastor's hand. The pastor can receive the people and direct them to the counselor. If the pastor speaks at length with a person who has come forward, it will cause some to delay coming forward and the conviction of the Holy Spirit will be interrupted. This insensitivity and lack of prepared counselors can make the invitation much less effective.

To give an effective invitation realize:

That Jesus calls every follower to openly and publicly confess him (Matthew 10:32-33); (Peter's Evangelistic Sermon—Acts 2:39-39); (Romans 10:9-10).

That a public profession of faith seals the commitment of new convert and gives assurance (Romans 10:9-10).

1.   That a public profession of faith gives the opportunity for a counselor to guide and give encouragement. .

2.   That the public profession of faith gives a strong witness for Christ to family, friends, acquaintances, and the people in the worship service.

To give an effective invitation make sure it is:

1. Spiritual: Depend on the Holy Spirit. Trust him to use the Word to convict those who are lost. Pray for God's anointing for the invitation. He is the one who draws people to Christ.

2. Clear: Tell the people what you are asking them to do. (Lift your hand; stand; come forward; by your coming you are confessing Christ as Savior and Lord; check your decision and sign the card you received.) Do not be vague. Do not say, "We will sing an invitation hymn and you may come." They may think, "Come for what?" Give clear instructions.

3. Confidence: You have biblical authority for extending the invitation. You have authority to call people to receive Christ. Ask them to receive Christ and make their commitment to follow him.

4. Focus: Make sure there are no distractions, like standing so the person in the middle of a row has difficulty moving to the aisle. You can begin the invitation while people are seated. Ask them to pray, receive Christ and stand and come forward while others are seated. They can more easily move to the aisle. Music can distract as well. It may be better for a choir, music team, or music leader to sing quietly as people are free to decide and respond. As you are about to begin the invitation, share with the people that this is the most important part of the service. Ask them to please not to leave until the invitation has concluded.

5. Positive: In your appeal, do not say, "If you want receive Christ and come forward, now is the time." Instead, be positive, "Receive Christ now. God is speaking to your heart, now come forward as quickly as we stand!"

6. Connection: Make sure that the invitation is connected to the sermon. As you come to the conclusion of the sermon, move naturally into an explanation the plan of salvation. Without abruptness, begin the appeal for people to respond to Christ. Make the invitation a natural and spiritual flow of the message.

7. Biblical: Use bible quotes that invite people to come to Christ. Examples are, "Whosoever will, let him come to me," Jesus said. "Come all who labor and are heavily laden and I will give you rest. Confess me before men and I will confess you before my Father in Heaven." There are many other biblical quotes you can use.

8. Brevity of Prayer: Pray briefly for God's spirit to work in hearts and for those who need to make a decision for Christ to do so. (A long prayer will often disrupt the invitation and the Holy Spirit's work in hearts may be interrupted.)

Possibilities for extending an invitation:

1. At the conclusion of the message, you may ask the people to bow their heads and close their eyes. Explain that some have never received Christ and committed their lives to him. "You may be religious, have a church membership, and have been baptized, but have never truly been born again. Or, you may have never had a church relationship. The key is to receive Christ. Right now, I am asking you to believe in Christ, repent of your sin, and pray to receive him.

"How do you receive him? Simply pray and ask him to come into your heart and life. You may ask, 'What do I say in prayer?' If you can mean this prayer, pray these words after me, *'Lord Jesus, I do believe in you. I know I am a sinner. Thank you for dying for my sins. Please forgive me of my sins. Come into my heart. I receive you as my Savior and Lord. Thank you for coming into my heart.'"* Those who prayed and are receiving Christ then come forward.

2. At the conclusion of your message, ask people to bow their heads and close their eyes. Ask, "How many of you know for sure that if you were to die today, you would be in heaven with Jesus? If you do, as a testimony for him please, lift your hand. Thank you for your testimony! Some could not honestly lift their hands. You know that Christ is not in your life. I ask you now to receive him. If you will, simply tell him now that you want him in your life. Then, as we stand, be the first to step out and come forward. We will pray with you as you receive Christ." Pray briefly and ask the people to stand and come as the music begins.

Public Proclamation Outside the Church's Facility

If public proclamation is to be effective in reaching the lost, we must either get the lost into the church where it is being done or take the public proclamation out to the lost.

Opportunities abound to do public proclamation to the lost. Multitudes of opportunities are out there to share the Gospel in the public arena. Where and how can the Gospel be preached outside of the church building?

Possibilities

1. Schedule a music or preaching event in a park or on a busy street corner. Get permission from the authorities for the event. Set up. Have music first with a brief testimony or two, then briefly preach the Gospel—no more than five minutes—and extend an invitation. Have counselors with marked New Testaments spread through the crowd. When people pray and receive Christ, ask them to lift their hands if they received Christ. Counselors move to their sides and congratulate and counsel them about their decision.

2. Crusades in stadiums and auditoriums. The evangelist you engage will have preparation and follow-up material for you to use.

3. Schools, colleges, and universities will often permit you to have an evangelistic meeting on their campuses with students allowed to come on a voluntary basis. Share the Gospel without a denominational slant. Ask people to bow and pray and receive Christ. Then lift their hands if they did so.

4. Funerals. I have led many to Christ while preaching a funeral. I talk about the person, then I tell the congregation that if the person in the coffin could speak, he or she would encourage us to prepare to meet our Lord. Then I share the Gospel and ask them to bow their heads and pray with me to receive Christ. I ask them to lift their hands if they did so. Then I instruct them to go to church on Sunday to a Bible-believing church and go forward and tell the pastor that they have received Christ and want to follow him. Through my ministry, I have seen hundreds of people receive Christ at funerals and then come to the church where I was pastor. At one service more than sixty people received Christ. On the following Sunday, 167 people made public decisions for Christ.

5. Weddings. Recently I did a wedding and the Christian couple asked me to present the Gospel and give an invitation during the ceremony. I did it. Several lifted their hands that they were receiving Christ.

6. Apartment complexes. You can have a Backyard Bible Club for children, and at the close each day have a general gathering of children, parents, and residents. Serve refreshments. Publicize it throughout the apartment complex. Before refreshments, sing a brief song that everyone knows, then share the Gospel and extend an invitation for people to receive Christ. I did this in San Francisco. We had many professions, including Rita from Columbia. Rita was gloriously converted and shared testimony. Apartment managers will usually welcome you. They want to provide good activities for their residents and provide guidance that will help them become more responsible.

7. Apartment complexes for senior adults. You can get permission to use the community room for a senior adult activity where refreshments will be served, the Gospel presented, and an invitation extended.

8. Businesses. Many business owners will be glad for you to come and speak to their employees briefly. Present the Gospel and extend an invitation.

9. Television and radio programs. These are available for purchase and in some communities they are complimentary as public service time.

Public proclamation is one of the five essential techniques given in the Book of Acts for a church to be effective in reaching the lost for Christ. Some lost people will come to the worship services for various reasons. If the other four evangelistic techniques are implemented, many people who need Christ will attend the worship services.

CHAPTER FOUR
Caring Ministry

Caring ministry is the second biblical technique found in the book of Acts that helps the church become effective in reaching the lost for Christ. Almost every church does caring ministry. However, some of them only do the ministry internally for members and have not reached out beyond their membership to those who need Christ. Certainly, we must minister to our own. If our members have special needs and are ignored by their own church, they may become disappointed and drop out. Some of these become "church casualties" who say things like, "I was hurting and needy and nobody at my church cared." Our churches must develop processes to enable us to stay in touch and know what is happening in the lives of our members. We must organize and put into action systems that will guarantee that someone will be responsible for ministering to *all* of our own people.

A church must care for its own members, but to reach the lost in the community it must care and minister to them. Caring ministry to those outside of our church does not automatically happen. While our members do care, they often do not know where to begin to reach out to the lost and non-churched in ministry. The church must lead in the emphasis of reaching out and ministering to them. This requires intentional planning for such ministries and assigning a member or group of members to be responsible for implementation. Some of our members have the heart and gifts to minister. Out of their love for Christ and for people they will naturally become involved in ministry.

Dorcas is a Biblical Example of Caring Ministry

A wonderful biblical example of caring ministry is Dorcas in Acts 9:36-42. "This woman was full of good works and charitable deeds which she did."

Dorcas became sick and died. Peter came to Joppa where the body of Dorcas lay in an upper room. When Peter entered, "all the widows approached him weeping, showing him the robes and clothes that Dorcas had made while she was with them." Peter spoke to her and said, "Tabitha, get up." She arose and Peter took her by the hand and presented Dorcas to her, alive! (Acts 9:39 HCSB)

Verse forty-two declares, "This became known throughout all Joppa, and many believed in the Lord."

Caring ministry opens the door to share the Gospel and lead many to Christ. It affirms the truth that Christ lives in us and his love flows through his people to minister to others. It breaks down barriers through actions that show his love. It forms a rapport and a relationship that opens hearts to the Gospel of Jesus and his salvation. In Joppa many believed because of the caring, Christ-centered ministry of Dorcas.

Dynamic of Caring Ministry

Legitimizes the Gospel and the Church's Ministry

The witness of individual believers, of churches, and of the Gospel is legitimized in the minds and hearts of the non-churched community by caring ministry wherever it happens. Our son and daughter-in-law, Loren and Kathryn, felt led of God to begin a new church in an area where their denomination, Southern Baptist Convention, was little known. They started with a small group meeting in their home. They were looked on almost like a cult. Their strong gift was that of mercy. They began to reach out to individuals in need. They provided food, clothing, shelter, and counsel. More and more needy people were attracted to them.

They began to reach the lost and non-churched. They rented a house and remodeled it for worship and Bible study. In time, the community began to accept them. They involved themselves in the life of the community. Today, they and their church are known as the "people who care and will help." Many in their church are people who had no church, but now they are believers and productive members.

Establishes Relationships to Reach the Deepest Need:
Two Levels of Need: Surface Level and Spirit Level

- The surface level includes physical, emotional, mental, and relational needs.

Through the surface level of caring ministry, believers get to know those outside the church. They develop a relationship and become friends. They begin to minister to surface needs like providing food, putting clothes on their backs and shoes on their feet, giving counsel and guidance for them to face their problems, and helping to them with their hurt. This is the obedient and joyful fulfillment of Jesus' words in Matthew 25:34-40 NKJV:

> **Then the King will say to those on His right hand, "Come, you blessed of My Father, inherit the kingdom prepared for you from the foundation of the world: for I was hungry and you gave Me food; I was thirsty and you gave Me drink; I was a stranger and you took Me in; I was naked and you clothed Me; I was sick and you visited Me; I was in prison and you came to Me."**

> **Then the righteous will answer Him, saying, "Lord, when did we see hungry and feed You, or thirsty and give You drink? When did we see You a stranger and take You in, or naked and clothe You? Or, when did we see You sick, or in prison, and come to You?"**

> **And the King will answer and say to them, "Assuredly, I say to you, inasmuch as you did it to one of the least of these My brethren, you did it to Me."**

We obey Jesus as we minister to people in their human, surface needs. But Jesus went further than the surface needs to minister at the point of people's deepest need, their spiritual need. He spoke the truth of God to them. We need to follow the model of Jesus to not only minister to people at the point of their surface need, but then to move on as the Holy Spirit opens the door to minister to them spiritually to share Christ and seek to lead them to Christ.

If we stop with the surface need, we become little different from persons involved in social work or governmental welfare programs. We have stopped short of the purpose of God. We can utilize ministry to surface needs and open the opportunity to lead the person or persons to Christ. This will do more to help them become stable and deal with their issues of life than any other thing. Often, the major reason for their problems is the fact that they do not know Christ and how to apply his truth as it applies to their lives and situations.

- The spirit level of caring ministry moves us from the surface level to minister to a person's spiritual need and to share Jesus with them.

This is a challenge that causes some to resist moving to the spirit level of meeting needs. Some will say such things like, "Our purpose is to meet human needs, get acquainted, build relationships, and gain their trust." Then, they hasten to say, "But we do not 'stuff the Bible down their throats.'"

Through my years of ministry, I have often heard the charge against those who consistently share Christ with people that they are "stuffing the Bible down their throat;" "twisting their arms;" "manipulating them." That wrong kind of approach can be taken. However, my observation after fifty-five years of pastoral and denominational leadership is that it is seldom done that way. In reality, lost people often wonder why Christians do not talk to them about Christ if their experience with him is genuine. Lost people are hurting and often long for a Christian to reach out to them with the loving and true message of Christ.

My question has been, "Do you share the Gospel of Christ and guide them to receive and follow Christ?"

Yes! We do need to be sensitive to "build a relationship." But the time it takes to build a relationship to the extent that we can effectively share Christ varies. It may take three years, three months, or three minutes for such a relationship to happen. It depends on the work of the Holy Spirit in the life of the person at that given point and our own sensitivity to the person and to the Spirit.

An intentional and relational witnessing approach in our caring ministry is imperative. Caring Ministry opens the door for the development of a meaningful relationship. Intentionality in witnessing as soon as there is openness in a person's heart requires spiritual sensitivity. Simply dialoguing with them and asking questions can open the door to share Christ in a natural and nonthreatening way (See Chapter Seven: Personal Presentation for more on this topic.)

This was illustrated by one of the finest soulwinners I have known, O. E. Wilkins. He was retired, and a deacon in our church. He didn't have enough to live on, so he took a job at a supermarket to supplement his retirement income. He was frail and not in good health. He worked until 3:00 PM each weekday. Our church asked him to be the team leader of our Benevolence Team. O. E. devoted three hours each day from 3:00 PM to 6:00 PM to that ministry. He would take the names of people who needed food and clothing and deliver it to them at their homes.

As his pastor, I trained him along with many others of our members to get the permission of the people to whom he ministered and read through John 3:1-18 with them. (I have included this dialogue in my book, *People Sharing Jesus and in the People Sharing Jesus New Testament*. It is also in Chapter Eight of this book.) O. E. made a practice of doing it.

On one occasion, he took food to a very needy family. Both husband and wife had lost their jobs. They were embarrassed, but thankful to take the food. O. E. asked permission to share John 3. They had never realized that they needed to be born again! The entire family prayed with O. E. and committed their lives to Christ. They were baptized and became active members of the church. People in the church helped them find jobs.

The husband and wife gave their testimony, which moved all of us to tears. They said, "We have always been independent and did not think we needed the church or anyone else. Then we lost our jobs and were in great need. The church came to us. Now we are saved and God has given us new jobs. We are so grateful that we lost our jobs and were without food. Otherwise we might not have ever come to know Christ and be a part of the church."

After I left the church to pastor in another place, the pastor who followed me called me to tell me about O. E. He was in failing health. The pastor said that O. E. was one of the most consistent soulwinners in the church. O.E. had learned that ministering to people and witnessing go hand in hand, and he said that he learned how to lead people to Christ when Brother Darrell taught him how to lead people through John 3:1-18. Indeed, ministering and witnessing go together.

Difficulties of a Caring Ministry

With every positive initiative of our lives and our churches, there are always difficulties with which we are faced. Some of them are quite large and discouraging, but can be overcome as we obey God's Word!

How do we help our people become involved in ministering and witnessing to people outside of the church? Many have so many problems themselves that they do not think of others. Others do not think there is anything they can do. Let me give a few suggestions.

1. Teach what is in the Bible, especially what Jesus says about ministering.

2. Lead a study on spiritual gifts. I have published a book on spiritual gifts called *Incredibly Gifted* for that purpose. In the book I describe how Ephesians 4:11-12 tells us that every Christian has the gift of ministry. Every one of us can minister in some way for Christ and to others.

3. Lead the church to investigate the ministries that are needed to help people in its community.

4. Ask the members to pray, search their hearts, and determine the ministries that appeal to them and how they might become involved. There is a ministry that will appeal to every Christian according to their particular gifts.

5. When God places a ministry on the heart of a member, allow and support him or her to begin that ministry. Continue to encourage them.

6. Start every ministry with the purpose of evangelism to reach people as the Holy Spirit gives openings. Teach the

ministering people to be genuine and not manipulative, but to look for opportunities to share the Gospel and lead them to Christ.

Every Christian has within themselves a compassion for those in need because Jesus lives in them. When we are yielded to Christ and the Fruit of the Spirit is in our lives, we will naturally care for others and desire to help.

Difficulty of Dealing with People in Need

Multitudes of people are genuinely in need. They usually need the church to reach out to them. A church should have systems for detecting the needs of people in its community so it can reach out to them. As a church does geographic saturation in its Jerusalem, it will discover people with varied needs. Through geographic saturation, our church discovered numerous language groups in our area. Through the years, it resulted in our starting Korean, Hispanic, Brazilian, Ethiopian, English as a Second Language, and other language ministries.

Some people, however, are not genuine and will seek to take advantage of the church or of the person ministering to them. How do we know if the person is genuine and the need is real?

Personally, from the time I read Jesus' word in Matthew 5:42 just after God called me to preach when I was seventeen years of age, I concluded that it is better for me to help someone who does not need it and is trying to use me than to risk not helping someone in real need. "Give to the one who asks you, and don't turn away from the one who wants to borrow from you"(Matthew 5:42 HCSB). As a result of Jesus' words, I have had people take advantage of me numerous times, but most of the time the ministering has been needed and meaningful. We must never become calloused and hardened toward people.

The insincere who try to take advantage have needs too. Often, what they ask for is not what they really need. They need spiritual guidance in their lives and we can minister to them at the point of their need.

To adequately minister to people, the gift of discernment is needed. This is the reason that the church is best qualified to do caring ministry. Members can work together as a team to minister in the best way. Someone on the team will have a gift of discernment.

It is good to establish boundaries, or needy people will consume us. They need to understand and respect our boundaries. This, too, can be a ministry of helping them to learn to respect others and live within boundaries. Some are driven by their own crises and want immediate gratification. We can help them to learn to wait on the Lord, trust in him, and guide them to take the actions in their lives that will make a difference as we minister to them.

People like my son, Loren, who has a gift of mercy, tend to draw needy people to themselves. I told him when he began to pastor, "You have a gift of mercy, and you will draw needy people to yourself. If you do not learn to establish boundaries and communicate them to the people to whom you are ministering, they will consume your time and energy. You will become ineffective as a pastor and will be dominated by people who demand your attention." It happened as I predicted, but Loren has learned to establish the boundaries and thus has been able to pastor effectively and help people grow in Christ.

Difficulty of Maintaining Priority in Caring Ministry

Our priority of caring ministry is to care and meet human need to minister to them at the point of their deepest need—leading them to Christ! But, the tendency of ministry is to move away from evangelism. When it does, people begin to do ministry for the sake of ministry and the fulfillment they get from doing the ministry. Many ministries have been begun with the priority of leading people to Christ. But eventually the ministry is caught up in the mechanics of doing the ministry. People find fulfillment in doing the ministry, but evangelism ceases to happen.

What can be done? Structuring the ministry is the answer. Build into the ministry the processes of evaluation and make sure that the priority of evangelism continues.

An example is a day care and kindergarten ministry that we started in a new church where I was pastor. The church facility was located just a half mile from an Air Force base. We started the church, but could not visit people in the village on base due to military regulations. God gave us the idea of starting a day care and kindergarten to draw the military people out to us. I think that it was the first of its kind in the Southern Baptist Convention. Many of the Air Force people appreciated this ministry and brought their children. Women in the church worked in the day care center at a low salary in order help the people in our military and to reach people for Christ.

When the Air Force people brought their children, it gave us the opportunity to visit in their homes and in the homes of others on the base. Our workers were soulwinners. Many on the base were reached for Christ and came to the church. Our new church led the association in numbers of baptisms.

Time passed. I moved to another church. The church with the day care center forgot that the priority of the day care center was to reach the lost for Christ. It began to minister for the sake of ministering and not to reach the lost for Christ. The ministry left its priority of evangelism. It became divisive in the life of the church and was ultimately abolished. Ministries must keep their priority of reaching the lost for Christ!

Examples of Ministries that Can Reach the Lost for Christ

Disasters Ministries

Ministering to people who experience need due to hurricanes, floods, fires, tornados and other disasters is a fine opportunity for a church to minister. A church can set up a disaster relief team who will be ready to call the church to action when a crisis happens. Preparing ahead is essential. To wait until it hits to act will be inadequate. Our area experienced hurricane Ike. Numbers of churches were prepared and immediately began to minister. They did a phenomenal job.

1. Benevolent Ministries

A church can set up a team of members to operate a ministry to distribute food, clothing, and household goods to those in need. The team should be trained to share the Gospel and lead those to Christ as the Holy Spirit opens the door. Church members can use their homes as a distribution center of necessities.

A wonderful older member of our church, Mrs. Butler, was a faithful witness for our Lord. When she and her husband were younger, they went every Sunday morning in their nice Cadillac to the nearby

Air Force base and picked up Air Force people. They brought them to Sunday school and church and then took them to their home and provided a good meal and a meaningful afternoon. They led many of those people serving our country to Christ.

In time, Mr. Butler died. Mrs. Butler was in ill health and was confined to a wheelchair. She no longer needed the Cadillac and sold it. Her garage was empty. She had a passion to reach the lost for Christ, but how could she do it? She decided to go through the phone book and call people whose names began with the letter "A" and go on through the alphabet.

She would call and say, "Hello, this is Mrs. Butler. You do not know me, but I felt led to call and ask you if you know Jesus." Some would hang up. Some would say angry words.

But some would say, "Oh, thank you Mrs. Butler. I need someone to talk to me about Jesus." She continued to share Jesus with people.

God gave her the idea of turning her garage into a ministry center. She had no need for it any longer. She got some of our men to build clothing racks and shelves. She made the church aware of her plan. Her home was near a poverty area. Our church members brought clothes, food, household necessities, and appliances to her garage. The word spread through the needy community that they could receive help at Mrs. Butler's home. She always shared Christ with them.

One morning, I received a call from Mrs. Butler. She asked if I could come and meet a young couple who were with her to receive food and clothing. When I walked in the door, she introduced me to the couple. She had led them to Christ. She said, "Pastor, this is Morris and Becky. Morris and Becky, this is *your* pastor!" They followed through with their decision. I baptized them and they grew in Christ. We can minister and lead people to Christ!

2. Counseling Ministries

Counseling ministries can range from Sunday school classes to reaching out to become a support group for people in distress to the church having a pastoral counselor on its staff.

A Sunday school class or support group in the church can used to support people in their emotional and marital needs. Some may say that they are not professionals and not qualified. However, often those with such needs will be helped through their difficulty by someone or some group who will reach out to them, accept them, and help bear their burden. Galatians 6:2 "Bear one another's burdens and so fulfill the law of Christ."

A men's Sunday school class who had a ministering teacher reached out to a prominent man in the community. John came to the class, but something seemed amiss. When John got in trouble at his job, he confessed to the class that he was a "closet alcoholic." The men accepted and loved him. They ministered to him and were available when he had a crisis of temptation to drink alcohol. Ultimately, John accepted Christ and was victorious over alcoholism.

Dr. Jay Adams in his book, *Competent to Counsel,* said "A Christian armed with the Word of God and filled with the Holy Spirit is competent to counsel."

When I was pastor at First Baptist Church in Pasadena, Texas, the church was growing and reaching all types of people. Some had intense problems. We came to believe that God wanted us to start a counseling center. We built a four-office building on the church property across the street from a hospital. We engaged Robert McGee as the director. His duties included to counseling those in need, training lay members to counsel and be a support team, educating our people about the need for counseling and how they can help, making sure the center continued to be Christ-centered and Bible-centered; and share the Gospel and leading people to Christ. He never manipulated people or forced the Gospel on anyone. They were to ask permission of the counselee before they shared the Gospel.

There are so many people in our churches and communities who have counseling needs that a church can never employ enough staff and counselors to meet all the needs. How can a church care for so many people? The entire church must become a caring, compassionate team committed to meet these needs.

Needless to say, many people were helped and many received support and Christ through the ministry of the church. In the years ahead, Robert McGee established the Rapha Counseling Centers that were greatly used of God in helping people.

3. Job Assistance Ministry

A church can set up a job assistance team to help those in need of a job. They can help them learn how to apply for a job and how to find job possibilities. They can study the area and identify companies and possibilities for jobs. This will be a great asset in communities with a high percentage of unemployed people.

A relatively small church in Arkansas reported one hundred twenty baptisms in one year through a job corps ministry. It assisted many in locating jobs, shared Christ with them, and continued to disciple them. People can be helped and led to Christ by meeting them at the point of their need.

4. Feeding the Homeless

Colleen saw the homeless and had a compassionate burden for them. She became a part of a caring ministry that provided breakfast for them in a park every Saturday. She helped serve the breakfasts, got acquainted with them, showed the love of Christ, gained their trust, and established a relationship. The Christian workers provided a van to take the homeless to church on Sunday.

Many homeless people feel trapped in their situation and need someone to care and guide them into a different lifestyle. They can be helped with their physical needs, get help finding a job and a place to live, and also find Christ.

A woman in Atlanta, Georgia, lived on the streets. Through a Crossover street ministry event, she received ministry and Christ. A year later one of the men involved in the Crossover event was speaking in a local church. This same woman came to him at the end of the worship service and told her story. After she received Christ, she came to the church, got a job, and a place to live. Her life had stabilized and she was living productively.

5. Ministries in the Church

Vacation Bible School (VBS) is one of the best ministries to reach children and their families. To have an effective VBS, the date needs to be set at least six months ahead so people can get it on their family calendar. Teachers and workers should immediately be enlisted. Two months ahead of the VBS the church should begin to promote it in the community through the mail, through saturation visitation, and signs in front of the church. The goal is to reach every child in the church's community. Every kind of temptation and danger is bidding for the lives of children: pornography, alcohol, tobacco, child molesters, homosexuality, atheism, cults, and many others. We must reach this generation of children in America. The Gospel needs to be shared with children in VBS and those who respond should be counseled. Follow up into the homes of non-churched children should be done by trained, witnessing church members.

AWANA is an excellent ministry to reach children and equip them with the Word of God.

Ministries to single adults are important for fellowship and caring provided by good activities where they can get together. Single women may need help with their cars. One church set up a monthly car service for them where they changed their oil and inspected the cars for possible problems.

Ministries to senior adults are needed. Senior adults are one of the most rapidly increasing groups in many of our communities. A church can provide for house and yard maintenance for senior adults. Seniors have incredible gifts. They can be active in evangelistic outreach, prayer ministries, helping with benevolence ministries, food service, helping families when there is a death or crisis, and many other responsibilities. They have time and great expertise. They need positive, productive involvement.

There are many non-English speaking people in our communities. What an opportunity for a church to provide classes to teach English. Almost all of them desire to learn English. Our church set up an ESL ministry, and we reached many through these classes. The success of this resulted in a Brazilian church and a Hispanic ministry.

There are multitudes of ministries that are a possibility for a church. Dr. Charles Rossell, Pastor of First Baptist Church in Leesburg, Florida, challenged his people to minister. He suggested that they pray and determine the ministry where God wanted them to be involved. Members would come to him with a ministry on their heart. If the church did not have such a ministry, he delegated to them to start such a ministry. The last time I spoke to him, his church had fifty-five ministries that involved his people and helped reach many for Christ.

6. Recreation Ministries

Children and families often respond enthusiastically to a church basketball program. Our church has numerous teams coached by members. Many parents, grandparents, friends, and neighbors come to the games on Saturdays. As I write this material, I have just returned from an Upward Basketball game where I shared the Gospel and invited people to pray and receive Christ during halftime at a game. Many people—including several adults—lifted their hands indicating that they had prayed with me to receive Christ.

One Sunday afternoon I was driving home from the lake. I passed a pickup truck pulling a boat. The truck was stalled. I stopped to help. Charlie, the driver, was perplexed. We could not fix it, so I gave Charlie a ride home. I visited with him and shared Christ with him. He was a hardened man! He refused to receive Christ, but said he would visit our church. Sometime later, I met Charlie in a grocery store. I greeted him. He was friendly. I said, "Charlie, we have a church softball team. We need a good ball player like you! Would you join our team?

He said, "Yes, I would like to play."

I said, "The requirement of the league is that you be in Sunday school and church two Sundays a month."

Charlie said, "I will do it." In the weeks ahead, Charlie did come to Sunday school and church and enjoyed playing softball. Our team surrounded him with acceptance and love.

Charlie came under conviction through the Holy Spirit. It was so heavy that he had to go one way or the other. Suddenly, he disappeared. His wife called to say that Charlie was missing. He had gotten drunk and gotten into a fight. The authorities were looking for him. The softball team and I prayed for him. Two days later, his wife, Evelyn, called to ask me to come to their house. She said, "Charlie is at home and he is saved!"

I went to their home. We prayed and rejoiced! As Charlie listened to the radio, Billy Graham came on the radio and Charlie prayed with him and received Christ. He had a job offer in a distant town, but he wanted to be baptized immediately. I called the church together on a Monday night. We baptized him and he went on to his job and transferred his membership to a church there.

We called John Tucker to be our minister of recreation at Dauphin Way Baptist Church in Mobile, Alabama. John used our outstanding center to be Christ-centered, Bible-centered, and Evangelistic. Through the recreation ministry multitudes came to know Christ.

These are examples of ministries that can be used to reach the lost for Christ. There are many others. Search for the ministries that God can use in your area to minister and reach people

Multitudes of ministries are possibilities for churches to use minister to people and lead them to Christ. Caring ministry will be synergistic, resulting in more lost people attending worship services for public proclamation.

CHAPTER FIVE
Event Attraction

An event attraction is where God does a mighty work. It has great possibilities for reaching the lost for Christ. Almost every church conducts events, but they are not always evangelistic events. Along with the other four biblical techniques (public proclamation, caring ministry, geographic saturation, and personal presentation), event attraction will add a strong dimension to a church's total strategy for evangelism.

The biblical example of event attraction where God does a mighty work is in Acts 3 when Peter and John went to the temple.

> Now Peter and John were going up together to the temple complex at the hour of prayer, at three in the afternoon. And a man who was lame from his mother's womb was carried there and placed every day at the temple gate called Beautiful, so he could beg from those entering the temple complex. When he saw Peter and John about to enter the temple complex, he asked for help. Peter, along with John looked at him intently and said, "Look at us." So he turned to them, expecting to get something from them. But Peter said, "I have neither silver nor gold, but what I have I give to you: In the name of Jesus Christ the Nazarene, get up and walk!" Then, taking him by the right hand he raised him up, and at once his feet and ankles became

strong. So he jumped up, stood, and started to walk, and entered the temple complex with them—walking, leaping, and praising God" (Acts 3:1-8 HCSB).

What a marvelous and mighty work of God. A large crowd was attracted. When God does a mighty work, it gets the attention of the people. Peter stood before them and explained what had happened in the name of Jesus. He preached Christ and charged them with killing the Son of God, the Prince of Life. Peter told them that the one they crucified, God had raised from the dead.

Peter called them to repentance and proved from the Old Testament prophets that had sent Jesus to "bless you by turning each of you from your evil ways" (Acts 3:26 HCSB). He gave an evangelistic invitation: "Therefore repent and turn back, that your sins may wiped out, so that seasons times of refreshing may come from the presence of the Lord" (Acts 3:19 HCSB).

"But many of those who heard the message believed, and the number of the men came to about five thousand" (Acts 4:4 HCSB).

Five thousand men, not including women and children, believed in Christ. What a mighty event that attracted people and resulted in their salvation!

Dynamic of Event Attraction

Churches can use events to attract those outside of the church to attend and hear the Gospel presented. When churches engage God-anointed men, women, groups, and presentations through which God has done a mighty work, the community will be interested and consider attending. However, many churches do conduct advents, but few lost people come. What can make a difference in the effectiveness of an event? Preparation is the key. Consider the following suggestions:

1. Schedule the event well ahead of time—a year ahead; not less than six months. Church members need to be involved. They are busy! Make sure they know about it and are able to place it in their personal and family calendars. Early planning is essential to budget adequately for its effectiveness. To engage the right personnel requires early planning.

2. Engage the personnel to lead the event attraction at the time you schedule the event.

3. Begin publicity within the church membership three months ahead of the event.

4. Plan for prayer and organize prayer teams, groups, and home prayer meetings well ahead of the event.

5. Train your people to witness and lead people to receive Christ three months ahead.

6. Saturate the community with information about the event. Begin one month before the event. Use signs, newspapers, letters to prospects, phone calls, and promotional leaflets.

7. Two weeks before the event begin door-to-door visitation to invite the people of the community to share Christ with them as the Holy Spirit leads.

8. Assign prospects to individual members for them to cultivate and bring to the event.

9. Train counselors to assist the pastor with those who make decisions. If the pastor alone tries to counsel each one, the harvest will be minimized and the invitation will be too long.

10. At the event, register every attendee. With everyone registering, guests will not feel that they are "on the spot" and singled out. Let the ushers hand out the registration cards to every attendee, then collect them row-by-row before dismissal. On the registration card give spaces for them to list their name, address, phone number, e-mail address, church membership and squares they can check such as: interested in the church; prayed to receive Christ; recommitted life to Christ; desire a visit.

11. Make sure the plan of salvation is presented and extend an invitation for a decision for Christ. The invitation may be a "come forward invitation" or a check box on the registration card.

12. Be sure to follow up with every guest. This is critical if you want to reach people!

The first level of follow up is by telephone, no later than two days after the event. Train a team of callers to: 1. Thank them for coming. 2. Ask if they are interested in the church. 3. Ask if they have come to know Christ as Savior and Lord or if they are still in the process. 4. If they do not know Christ, ask permission to share the Gospel and seek to lead them to Christ while you are on the phone. 5. Ask if you can make an appointment to come to their home to get better acquainted and share more about Jesus.

The second level is a home visit to each person who does not have a church home. Visit and share the Gospel if they do not know Christ

When I was pastor at Dauphin Way Baptist Church in Mobile, Alabama, we conducted an event attraction at Christmastime—a Christmas special. We did the things listed above. Many guests came and filled out registration cards. We made telephone calls no more than twenty-four hours after they attended. We distributed the cards to staff and witnessing members.

On Saturday morning before Christmas my wife, Kathy, and I went through our stack of cards for follow-up visits. We prayed and left home to arrive for the first visit at about 9:30 AM at the home of Bob and Patty. We did not know them, but knocked on the door. Breathlessly, Patty came to the door. We could smell the bacon and knew that this was too early. We introduced ourselves and I apologized. "Patty, we have come too early. Let us come back a little later."

Patty laughingly responded, "You should have seen me dress in my robe as I saw you getting out of your car. I am a fast-change artist! But, no, you must not go away. Do come in. We were just talking about while we had coffee!"

Inside, Bob and Patty were effusive in telling us how they enjoyed the Christmas music and the entire event. I shared the plan of salvation in about four minutes and gave an invitation for those who prayed with me to check the square on the registration card. They complimented me on my presentation. As we visited, we found that they went to church sometimes, but had no church home. I asked, "Have you come to know Jesus in a personal way, or would you say you are still in the process?"

Both of them said that they were still in the process. I said, "Then you have been thinking about it?"

"Yes, we have been thinking about it a lot." We continued talking, and Bob and Patty prayed with us and received Christ. I explained Baptism and how to follow Christ by continuing to grow in him.

Then I said, "I hope you will come to Dauphin Way tomorrow."

They were joyful when they responded, "Yes we will be there in the morning. We will join Dauphin Way Baptist Church. After all, who in Mobile, Alabama would be out sharing Jesus with people on the Saturday before Christmas but you Baptists. We will be there!"

Now, I have heard other things said about Baptists and our home visitation. What a delight and encouragement Bob and Patty were to us and the entire church. I did baptize them and they became very active witnesses for Christ and leaders in the church.

Event attraction does work when it is prepared for and done effectively by God-anointed people. It can involve the total church in preparation, reaching out to friends and neighbors, actually conducting the event, doing counseling, working on the parking lot to direct traffic, greeting people, ushering, visiting and inviting, telephoning, and making follow-up visits.

It must be a Holy Spirit filled and God-anointed event with personnel who are used of God. But it also, requires effective planning, organization, and implementation.

When this happens, event attraction is dynamic!

Difficulties of Event Attraction

There are certain difficulties that plague the use of event attraction as an evangelistic technique to reach the lost for Christ. Satan desires for us to get sidetracked from our priority to reach the lost. He works in the area of how we conduct evangelistic events. Some of these difficulties are:

1. The tendency to take the easy route and not make the event distinctively evangelistic. Many churches conduct events and expect the lost to attend and be saved. But they do not do the necessary preparation. They simply set the event on the church calendar and do not prepare to reach the lost. They think that they have done what they need to do by scheduling the event. I promise you, the lost will not come if they do not know about

47

it. There is a tendency to drift away from rather than toward evangelism in our events.

2. Depending on the world and the flesh rather than the Holy Spirit for the effectiveness of the event will short-circuit its effectiveness! Churches can become superficial and synthetic in trying to produce a mighty work of God. We cannot produce it in the flesh. We can resort to engaging personnel to lead the event who are not God-anointed and are superficial to attract a crowd. They know how to get a crowd! This is sensationalism. The problem is that in the desire to get the crowds, we do things that are unbiblical and even unethical to reach the crowds. The problem is that we see someone or a group that is effective in getting the crowds. We invite them to help us because we want to attract crowds, but we do not know about their spiritual lives. We invite them. They attract the crowds not because they are spiritual, but because they are popular. They know how to get crowds and they do. But they play on the emotions and are superficial and not spiritual. God cannot bless this spiritually.

3. When it departs from the evangelistic purpose of the event, a church can conduct a fine event, yet fail in sharing the Gospel and leading people to Christ. I had the experience of attending an excellent Christmas event that is an example. It was at a larger, prominent church. The event was a "living Christmas tree." It was excellent, but the Gospel was not shared. No invitation was given. When it ended, the pastor said, "This is our Christmas gift to our community. Have a Merry Christmas. Good night! I left with emptiness in my heart.

4. Be careful not to conduct events in isolation from the church's understanding of the strategy of total evangelism. Use caring ministry, geographic saturation, and personal presentation to enhance both the attendance and evangelistic effectiveness of the event.

God forbid that we waste God's money, the church's time, and our time by not preparing well and making the event biblically evangelistic. Events can be productive in ministering and reaching people. Simply having an event for the sake of having an event is inadequate. They may be enjoyable, yet non-productive. Events should be planned to fulfill the church's priority and strategic vision. The question is, "What types of events can be used to fulfill the church's evangelistic priority?"

Events That Can Be Evangelistic

- Church Revivals: When I was vice president for evangelism for Southern Baptists at the Home Mission Board, I attended a pastor's meeting. Dr. W. A. Criswell was there. He asked me, "Darrell, are revivals passé today? Do they work today?"

  My answer was, "That all depends, Dr. Criswell. It depends on three things: 1. Preparation we are willing to make. 2. The personnel we utilize. God has given the gift of the evangelist. To use a good evangelistic harvester and evangelistic musician is essential to reach people. Pastors swapping pulpits with their favorite pastor friend seldom is effective. 3. The follow up we are willing to do. These three things can make revivals successful today. "

Then he asked another question that I chose not to answer, "Why does my staff cringe and react negatively when I say that we need to have a revival?"

I asked others to give their input, although I thought I knew the answer. Knowing Dr. Criswell, I thought, "Dr. Criswell probably suggests in February that they need to have a revival in April. If it happened that way, staff already had a fully-planned schedule on the church calendar. To sandwich in a revival would interfere with things that were already in the process and the revival would be ineffective. They knew the value of early planning and preparation."

Using the gifted evangelist is a key. God has given the gift of the evangelist to people. They have the gift of encouraging the church and stimulating them to reach the lost. They are harvest oriented and can "draw the net" in reaching the lost for Christ. They are harvest evangelists. Through the years of my pastoral ministry, I averaged having a harvest evangelist every year of my ministry.

Revivals do still work and are needed if the three essentials mentioned above are done.

- Evangelistic Crusades: These may be done by an individual local church or a group of churches. They may be done in the church building or in a football stadium, park, tent, gymnasium, city auditorium, baseball stadium, and other places. I have helped conduct crusades in all of these kinds of places. People will come to them who would not come to the church building.

- Evangelistic Harvest Days: These may be done on Sundays. The same essentials of preparation, personnel, and follow up are necessary for them to be effective.

- Vacation Bible School: VBS is both a ministry and an event. It is one of the best Evangelistic Events a church does all year.

- Age Group Events such as:

1. Children's Carnival: I assisted in one of these for a church that had very few children, but wanted to reach their community and the children who lived there. Senior adults set up booths for dart throws, basketball shooting, and moon-walks. We served hot dogs and soft drinks. There was singing on a platform and someone shared a testimony or presented the Gospel and invited the crowd to join our church. Trained witnesses gave out marked New Testaments and went through the marked passages in Romans to share the Gospel. All of this was free. The only requirement was for the children to have a ticket for each activity. They received tickets as they entered and gave their names, addresses, phone number, and church preference. Their information card was put in a jar and a drawing was held periodically for a prize. Businesses contributed the prizes. People accepted Christ. One young mother said, "Thank you for doing this. Our community needs this kind of thing. When will you do it again?" Follow up was done and more children and parents began to attend the church and Sunday school.

2. Hallow Him at Halloween Time: Our son, Loren, served on the staff of the state convention of Baptists in Indiana. He and his family lived in suburban Mooresville near Indianapolis. Loren tells his story about Hallow Him.

"We sought ways to be involved with our church family and to reach out to our neighbors with the Gospel. In the fall we began to think about Halloween and how we could use that day as a witness for Christ. We had struggled with what to do, since its hyped-up themes are often scary, gory, and occultic. We didn't want to close our doors to the many children who would come by our house. We thought, 'How can we redeem this night, use it for God's glory, and share Jesus with the children and their parents?

"My wife, Kathryn, and I chose a fun theme for our costumes. We chose a 50s theme. Kathryn and Kimberly, our first child, dressed in poodle skirts and I wore blue jeans and white t-shirt. With a background of 50s music we gave candy, Gospel tracts, notes of our testimonies, an explanation of what we were doing, and an invitation to our church. We gave hot chocolate and cider to reluctant parents who stood nearby as we explained that we were celebrating Hallow Him to hallow the most hallowed one, Our Lord Jesus Christ.

"It was amazing to have over 125 children and parents come to our home. In the five years we lived in Mooresville, the event attracted about two hundred youth and adults each year. This gave us an open door to share Jesus with several families in our neighborhood.

"God moved on our hearts to start a new church on the east side of Indianapolis in New Palestine. We began New Faith Community Church in our home with ourselves, and three daughters, Kimberly, Natalie, and Olivia. By then 'Hallow Him' had become a tradition with our family. Our girls looked forward every year to 'Hallow Him,' and actually did not know the world called it Halloween. Someone would greet them with 'Happy Halloween.' The girls would correct them and say, 'You mean Happy Hallow Him, don't you?'

"The first year in New Palestine we chose the theme, *The Wizard of Oz*. I dressed as the Tin Man; Kathryn as the Scarecrow; Kimberly as Dorothy; Natalie as the Glinda the Good Witch; and Olivia as a little Munchkin. I built the Emerald City out of a refrigerator box and painted it green. We added popcorn to our menu. We spread invitations through the community and waited for them to come and give us an opportunity to share Jesus with our neighbors. It was a little disappointing when only fifty showed up.

"However, we made a huge impact on a young couple and their little girl. They were going through difficult circumstances and had moved in with the man's parents. The husband, Craig, had a rebellious spirit and had not been open to the Gospel. The wife, Lisa, was a believer and soon came to our church.

"The next summer, God opened the door of opportunity for me to share Jesus with Craig. After a heated argument with Lisa, Craig stormed out of the house and walked ten miles to the next town. 'He headed to the pool-hall!' Lisa told me on the phone. She asked me if I would go get him. I found him walking toward the pool hall, pulled up beside Craig, and asked him to get in. He was sun-burned and worn out. With his defenses gone, he was ready. We talked about how Jesus could transform his life and his marriage. As a result of Hallow Him, I had the privilege of leading Craig to Christ, which resulted in a new direction for him and his family."

Some of our "Hallow Him" Themes

50s

Western or cowboys

The Flintstones

Native American Indians

Medieval royal family (king, queen, and princesses)

The Wizard of Oz

Pioneer family (The Ingalls from *Little House on the Prairie*)

The circus

Disney characters (Drive-in Movie complete with cardboard cars and a big TV with Disney movies playing)

Hospital (doctors and nurses)'.

Your creativity can make this an effective evangelistic event for your family or church family. We have encouraged families in our church to do Hallow Him in their neighborhoods. If a church took this idea and enlisted and trained families to have a Hallow Him at their homes, it could saturate many neighborhoods with the message of Jesus at Halloween time. And the people enjoy doing it.

Evangelistic events such as "Hallow Him" never take the place of personal presentation of the Gospel, but are launching pads for believers to share the Gospel with those who attend the event. It is important that each person who participates is equipped to share Jesus.

3. Youth Evangelistic Events:

Youth-led weekend revivals

Youth music events

Pizza parties with music and an evangelistic message

A Saturday night youth rally with music, testimonies, and an evangelistic message.

4. Single Adult Events:

Single adult music concerts

Single adult retreats

Single adult dinner with evangelistic speaker

5. Young Adult Evangelistic Events:

Marriage enrichment retreat

Dinner with childcare provided

Valentine sweetheart banquet

6. Median Adult Events:

Empty nest

Aging parents

Preparing for retirement

Valentine sweetheart banquet

Gospel singing group

7. Senior Adult Events:

Gospel singing group

Senior adult revival

Senior adult game day

Senior adult luncheon

Senior adult training such as: will-making; exercise program for seniors; Bible passages for seniors

8. Evangelistic Events for Men:

Evangelistic fish fry

Wild game party

Special Christian athlete speakers

9. Evangelistic Events for Women:

Evangelistic tea time

Special women's speaker

10. Biblical Drama: Some of the most moving evangelistic services I have attended were when biblical dramas were given. One of the greats is Jim McNeal of St. Louis, Missouri, who has memorized entire books of the Bible and presents them as the biblical character who wrote them. He is a harvest evangelist. Another is Clyde Anandale of Atlanta, Georgia. He is dresses for the part and plays the role of biblical characters like James, John, Paul, and others while giving an effective invitation for the lost to come to Christ.

11. Special Evangelistic Films: A fine pastor led his church to have a showing of the film Fireproof in the worship center at his church. They prepared by prayer, publicizing, and assigning prospects to members to invite. The people became very involved in reaching non-churched friends and acquaintances. The result was a large attendance of lost people. Through follow up, new prospects were reached. The film was a bridge to reach many who had never attended a church service. There are many evangelistic Christian films that can be used. The Billy Graham organization has many options.

- Evangelistic Events at Holidays:

(1). New Year's Eve Event—with an emphasis on "beginning the New Year right." Publicize it thoroughly through the community. Many people sit alone that night, some are overwhelmed with depression, and others go to the wrong places. We need to provide a righteous alternative. You can have music, testimonies, Bible Study, prayer times, special speakers with messages, food, and fellowship. We did this in the churches where I was pastor. We would have the various activities from 7:00 PM until midnight and pray the New Year in.

One New Year's Eve, Charles, an engineer at NASA, and his family came. He had no church home. He got acquainted with the people and loved it all. He accepted Christ. His testimony was that he had always been drunk at the New Year. He said, "I determined that I would not be drunk this New Year, so I came to church. It changed my life!"

(2). Valentine banquets as evangelistic events, I love my church day as an emphasis on being the bride of Christ.

(3). Easter Evangelistic Events: Easter music events; Easter drama; special sermons; special speakers; celebrity testimony; and many other possibilities may be done. Capitalize on the fact that more people think about going to church on Easter Sunday than any other time. Do two weeks of community witness saturation and invitation before Easter. Make the service dynamic, but not long. Lead the church in prayer preparation for the service. Schedule a Baptism Service for Sunday night. It is special to many to be baptized on Easter.

(4). Mother's Day Event: Make it an emphasis on "the Christ-centered home."

(5). Memorial Day Event: Emphasize "the price of our freedom" nationally and spiritually in Christ. Invite every present and former military person in the community. Enlist a military person to preach or give testimony or sing at the service. Present the Gospel and give an invitation.

(6). July 4th Event: Emphasize "God and country" with a focus on patriotism and God's power in establishing our country. Invite all elected and public officials in the community.

(7). Labor Day Event: Emphasize "the dignity of work." Ask a lay person to share about their call to live for Christ in the work place. Invite workers and management in your community.

(8). Thanksgiving Event: Emphasize "the grace of gratitude" and invite the non-church people of the community for a free Thanksgiving dinner after the Sunday service. Church people can serve.

(9). Christmas Event: Conduct a "Christmas Special" that involves children, youth, and adults in music, drama, and sharing. Any church, small or large, can have an effective Christmas event and people who need Christ will come. Invite the community.

- Law Enforcement Event: Invite all those in the community who work in law enforcement. Recognize and honor them. Have a special prayer for them. Secure a God-anointed law enforcement person to speak or give testimony.

- Fire Department Event: Secure a fire department person to speak, give testimony, or sing. Invite all those in the community who are related to the fire department.

- Back to School Event: Emphasize appreciation for students, school teachers, and administrators. Secure a school person to have a part in the worship service. Invite all teachers in the community to attend. Find out the names and addresses of all the new teachers and administrators in the community and invite them. Serve them lunch after the church service.

- Community Block Party Event: Serve food, have games, music, and a brief evangelistic message. It could be a community fish fry or a community barbeque.

- Friday Night Singing Event: Have it in a gymnasium or fellowship hall. Serve refreshments. Enlist several singers in the community to perform. Ask those who desire to sing or play an instrument to volunteer. Share the Gospel and give an invitation. The music minister, Dan Sampson, did this effectively in our church. The attendance was great. Lost people came and even sang or played.

• Friend Day Event: On a Sunday morning emphasize "friendship with God and others." Promote and pray. Enlist every member from children to Senior Adults to bring them a friend who has not been in church. Statistics tell us that the majority of non-churched people who start going to church do so because *a friend invited them.*

Evangelistic event attraction has greater benefit to a church than just what happens at the event. First, it helps to create a climate of evangelism in the church. It influences church members to think about the spiritual condition of family, friends, neighbors, and associates at work, fellow students, and even casual contacts. We are living in a time of religious syncretism and pluralism. The doctrine of universalism is a creeping paralysis in churches of America. Universalism is the belief that ultimately all people will be saved. No one will finally be lost and go to hell.

Many Christians have lost sight of lostness. I heard Dr. Roy Fish say, "Although few people in church would confess that they believe in universalism theologically and doctrinally, they practice universalism in their lives." They live with lost family members, friends, neighbors, associates at work, and fellow students at school with no thought that they are lost! They let them live and die without Christ and go to hell with no thought of leading them to Christ and eternal life. Evangelistic events fan the flame of spiritual concern for the lost.

Second, evangelistic events involve church members in being trained and equipped to witness for Christ as they prepare for the event. Members are trained in preparation for the event to counsel with those who make decisions for Christ. Many develop the concern to pray for those who are lost to be saved. Others are trained and influenced toward evangelism in other ways.

These members grow spiritually and continue to do what they have been equipped to do. They continue to do it in the continuing life of the church.

Third, many lost and non-churched people are discovered and become known prospects for the witness of the church. The church continues to contact and minister to them. Although they did not make decisions during the event, they are likely to come to Christ and the church in the future.

Like a farmer, we sow the seed, but the harvest does not come immediately. We cultivate. God nurtures the Gospel seed and a harvest comes later. Paul wrote, "So we must not get tired of doing good, for we will reap at the proper time if we don't give up" (Galatians 6:9 HCSB).

Fourth, evangelistic events help to create a God consciousness in the community. As God does an impactful work through the event, the community is influenced toward God. They begin to think about God as they go about their daily lives. As a pastor, I justified our involvement in an area-wide crusade by telling our church people that if I knew we would not get one member through our participation, I would still favor our participating. I said that periodically our community needs to experience a "big splash for God" that will call their attention to Jesus Christ. Evangelistic events do that! They help create a God consciousness in the community. As a result, people begin to think about God and the need of their spiritual lives.

Fifth, evangelistic events assist witnessing church members in sharing Christ with their lost friends and acquaintances. Often those who are lost are fearful of church worship services and will not come to a regular service. Believers share Christ with them, but the lost persons are resistant. They know that if they receive Christ, they will be expected to be in church. When the church conducts a special evangelistic event, it gives the witnessing believer an opportunity to invite them to something special at the church building. They will often come with the believer. The effective event becomes a bridge and reinforces the witness of the believer. As the Gospel is presented, another Gospel seed is sown in their hearts and minds. They become more comfortable with being in the church building. Through the combined influence of the witness of a believer and the evangelistic event, the Holy Spirit brings conviction and they receive Christ and follow him.

Event attraction is a part of an overall strategy of a church to implement total penetration of its community with the Gospel. The objective of the church for total penetration is to share with every person the claims of Christ on his or her life in such a way that each can understand the Gospel and respond to him as Savior and Lord! A continuing harvest of souls will follow.

"Remember this: the person who sows sparingly will also reap sparingly, and the person who sows generously will also reap generously" (2 Corinthians 9:6 HCSB).

Event attraction will combine synergistically with caring ministry to enhance the attendance every Sunday at the public proclamation services.

CHAPTER SIX
Geographic Saturation

Acts 1:8; Acts 5:28; Acts 8:4; Acts 19:10

"**B**ut you will receive power when the Holy Spirit has come upon you; and you will be My witnesses in Jerusalem, in all Judea and Samaria, and to the ends of the earth" (Acts 1:8 HCSB).

Jesus commissioned the little group of disciples to implement total evangelism to take the Gospel and witness to every person in their world in that generation. He mentioned Jerusalem first. Why? That was where they were! You can't witness where you are not! You must start where you are. Yet I speak to many people who care about the lost in Africa and South America and think they would be great witnesses if they were there. But they never speak a word to witness to people in their neighborhood, at work, or at school. Something is wrong with that! We must start where we are!

That is exactly what the church in Acts did. They started where they were. Their task was impossible. They were so few. They were so ordinary. Their task was so overwhelming. But the Holy Spirit came and empowered them. They did what Jesus said and the Gospel permeated Jerusalem, overflowed through Judea, spread through Samaria, and extended to the end of the earth.

Luke tells the story of the spreading of the Gospel in Acts. It permeated Jerusalem in a short time. How do we know? The Sadducees who opposed Jesus and the church in Acts 5:28 HCS said, "And look, you have filled Jerusalem with your teaching, and are determined to bring this man's blood on us." The disciples did what Jesus said and saturated Jerusalem.

There seemed to be a problem in the church in Jerusalem. They had selective hearing! They heard Jesus tell them to witness in Jerusalem and Judea, but the missed what he said about witnessing in Samaria and to the end of the earth. They were content to stay in Jerusalem and Judea. They were successful! But it appears that they had no intention of going to Samaria to witness.

Satan attacked the young church with persecution to try to destroy it and its witness. Peter and John were imprisoned and forbidden to speak any more in the name of Jesus Christ. Stephen was stoned to death. Satan made a strategic error. He attacked and intended to destroy the church, but God caused his strategy to boomerang and open the door for the dynamic spread of the Gospel.

Luke tells us that because of the stoning of Stephen "Saul agreed with putting him to death. On that day a severe persecution broke out against the church in Jerusalem, and all except the apostils were scattered throughout the land of Judea and Samaria"(Acts 8:1 HCSB).

Acts 8:4 HCSB tells us, "So those who were scattered went on their way proclaiming the message of good news." (The word used here is *evangelizing.*)

Do you enjoy camping out to hunt, fish, or just enjoy the woods? When you camp out, you build a campfire to keep you warm and to cook your food. When you break up camp to leave, what do you do with the fire? You cover it with dirt or you quench it with water until the embers have no fire. You do not kick the fire. Satan wanted to put out the fire of the church, but he made a strategic error. *Satan kicked the fire.* It scattered! Everywhere an ember landed, a fresh fire started. Revival came and the Gospel spread.

The church scattered and the fire spread. Christians went everywhere evangelizing. Phillip went down to Samaria and preached Christ to them. Great revivals broke out in Samaria and many were saved.

Geographic saturation was happening!

Paul went to Ephesus and preached in the synagogue for three months. Some believed, but others were angered and drove Paul out from the synagogue. He went to downtown Ephesus to a school owned by Tyrannus. He reasoned and dialogued with people about Christ every day. "And this went on for two years, so that all the inhabitants of the province of Asia, both Jews and Greeks, heard the word of the Lord" (Acts 19:10 HCSB).

This was phenomenal! How did it happen? Paul reasoned daily with people about Jesus. One by one, people received Christ and Paul taught them to do what Jesus told him to do—witness for Christ. They did what Paul did and what Paul taught them to do and within two years time every person in Asia heard the word of Jesus. The church of Ephesus was one of the greatest in Christian history.

Geographic saturation was spreading!

A church commits to share Jesus with every person in its Jerusalem.

Acts 1:8 is Jesus' strategy for reaching the world. It begins with the church's "Jerusalem," its primary ministry area (PMA). It begins with each local church making the commitment to reach every person in its Jerusalem with the Gospel of Christ. This is a commitment to implement total penetration.

Sharing Jesus with them begins with discovering them. Most of them will never come to the church building and services. Jesus went to the home of Zachaeus in Jericho. Zachaeus was saved and his life changed. The religious people, the Sadducees and Pharisees, attacked Jesus and tried to discredit him for going to the home of a sinner. Jesus told them, "For the Son of Man has come to SEEK AND TO SAVE the lost" (Acts 19:10 HCSB). Jesus went where he was and found Zachaeus and saved him. Even Jesus had to find people before he could save them. We must do the same today. People reach people. We build buildings and have worship services, but few lost people come. If we reach the lost, we like Jesus must go find them as the first step in reaching them.

Define Your Jerusalem (Your PMA) for Witness

Each local church should define a definite geographic area or areas of influence for total penetration with the Gospel. The pastor and church should claim this area for Christ in prayer and accept the responsibility for sharing Christ with every person in that area, personally, in the power of the Holy Spirit. As a pastor, it was my conviction that I was accountable for the spiritual condition of every person within the area of our church. Not only is it the responsibility of the pastor, but the church shares that accountability.

Step-by-Step Procedure

Step #1. Locate the church building on a map.

Step #2. Estimate the radius of influence of the church. Extend a radius line on the map in each direction. The lines may extend out as far as the majority of members live or as far out as the area where people are who might decide to come to the church services.

Step #3. Draw a line around that area. Accept the responsibility of sharing Christ with every person in this primary area of witness for the church. Realize that God has given the pastor and people of your church the responsibility and accountability for the spiritual well-being of every person in this area.

Step #4. Saturate the primary area with the Gospel. Share Jesus with every person in that circle and present the claims of Christ on his or her life. Record the information you have obtained about them for your church's prospect file. Begin with the people in the house next door to the church building. Continue to extend the witness on out from the place of beginning. You probably will not be able to contact everyone with one attempt. You will need to saturate repeatedly. If your area is large, you could divide your area into zones and cover a zone each month, or at a predetermined interval. Of course, some will not be home, so you will need to go back to contact the homes you missed.

Step #5. Gradually enlarge your circle of intentional witness. The circle of primary influence should become an ever-growing circle. People in your area will receive and follow Christ. They will reach out to family and friends outside the primary ministry area.

Step #6. Plan and work as though your church were the only church in the area. If there are other churches in the same general area, you may have overlapping circles of influence. Is this good or bad? It is good! It is positive! We are not competing, but we are complementing one another in witness. We are engaged in kingdom work, not simply in the work of growing our own local church. If every church is doing what it should be doing, they will be doing the same thing—saturating their area with the Gospel and sharing Jesus with every person. Their circle of witness will overlap yours and each others. The witness will be powerful! This will be super-saturation. It will intensify the God consciousness throughout the area. It will create a climate for evangelism where people will come under conviction and begin to seek the Lord.

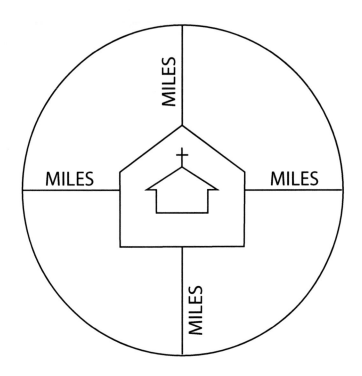

Overlapping circle of influence of several local churches

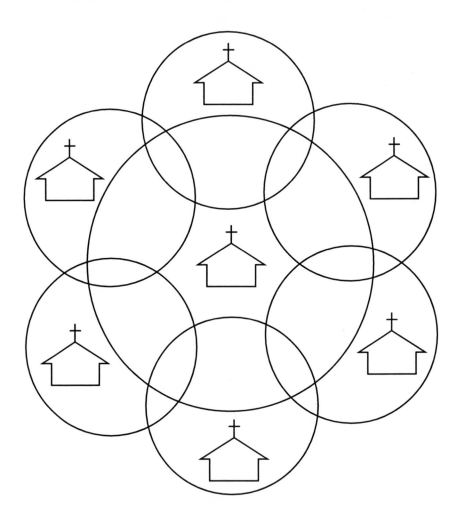

Geographic Saturation is Happening and it Works

Jesus' strategy for a church to reach its Jerusalem works. It worked in the first century in Jerusalem, Ephesus, and everywhere churches were started! It works today in the twenty-first century. It is a new paradigm two thousand years old. It is new because many do not do it.

It is two thousand years old because Jesus told us to do it two thousand years ago. While many do not do it and think it is outdated, many churches are doing it.

After I taught saturation evangelism in a church in a major city, the pastor wrote to me and said that it had changed his life. He said that he had never seen his community. He would drive through and never see the people. But, he said, "Now, I drive through and see every house and think about who lives there. I am filled with concern about our Jerusalem."

A fabulous story happened in Oakland, California. Pastor Newton Carey read my book, *Total Church Life,* which includes a chapter on saturation evangelism. He called his church together. Truevine Baptist Church in the community of Truevine had thirty-five members and met in the church building surrounded by a crime-ridden, drug-saturated, dangerous community. Newton told them that they were "an army for God to take Truevine for Christ." He explained his vision to take the Gospel to the streets and share Jesus with every person. His wife, Sally, trained the people to witness.

Truevine Church came together for prayer. Newton asked them all to get on their knees around a map of the community. He had outlined it with a marker. They prayed over the map and claimed Truevine Community for Christ. Then they got up and marched around the community praying every step of the way, claiming their Jerusalem for Christ. It was like Joshua and Jericho. They did it a second time. They began to witness. The Baptist missionary for that area was instrumental in getting marked New Testaments for them to use in witnessing.

Reports began to come to me about many being saved through Truevine's witness. First, the report was three hundred; then five hundred; then one thousand. Finally, it was reported that five thousand people had been saved. The church services grew until they were having several services every Sunday. Then they started services on Saturday nights and Friday nights. Finally, they secured a warehouse building and used it for worship and ministry.

The state sent in an investigative team to find out why the drug pushers had left Truevine community. I was scheduled to preach at the annual convention in that area, so Kathy and I went early to visit Truevine and see what was happening. When we parked in the parking lot, a man with a nametag, Joe, hurried out and opened the car doors for us. He welcomed us and escorted us into the worship service. I said, "Joe, how long have you been at Truevine?"

He replied, "About two years."

I asked, "How did you get here?"

Joe said, "I was taking drugs and was a drug pusher on the streets. They came and got me! I have been here ever since!"

Joe further shared, "I am from Michigan. When God changed my life, I wanted to go home to Michigan, but God would not let me. He said, 'Joe, the street you messed up, you got to go straighten up!'" Joe did help straighten up the streets. He went out and found other people he had sold drugs to and brought them into the church. He shared Christ with other drug pushers.

Geographic Saturation Works Today

Why should a church do geographic saturation?

First, this is Jesus' strategy. In Acts 1:8 he tells local churches to share Christ with every person in its Jerusalem and to not overlook any person. This is his purpose! He designed it!

Second, it cooperates with the way God works! Sooner or later, every person in the church's community will think, "God, I need God!" God works in people's lives to bring them to the point of thinking "God!" It may be through blessings, reversals, sickness, death, financial success, financial reversal, or births to bring them to the point of a realization that they need God. When they think God, it should not have been long since someone from the church touched their life in a positive way for Christ and the church.

If we have touched their life for Christ and in the name of the church, when they think "God," they will think about the church that touched their life. They will show up in church on Sunday or they will call the pastor or the member who touched their life. We will have an opportunity to reach them.

We need to have a touch on every life in our community at least every six months. How? Through a visit to the home, a phone call, a note left on the door, a letter or mail-out, or saturation leaflet left on the door, we can have a touch on their lives to remind them of Christ and the church.

Our church was practicing this very thing. We went to a neighborhood near the government installation of NASA. We went door-to-door. They were very unresponsive. Many turned us away. One man met me at the door and told me that he had problems with the Bible. He said it had inconsistencies. He was a genius. The reason I knew this was that he told me that he was a genius.

We decided not to go to every door every six months, but to go every three months. We did it and in the next year that was the most productive area in all our community. We reached more people from that area than any other.

It is interesting that many churches have forsaken Jesus' model of saturation evangelism when corporate America has adopted it for their secular and financial purposed. I fly on airplanes much of the time. Every time I fly, the plane is filled with company employees who are flying to meet clients in behalf or their company to sell a service. They could call on the phone; send an e-mail; or have a telephone or televised conference. They did not. They know that the personal touch makes the difference. They pay mega-bucks to have personal contact with their clients.

In a book on success in real estate sales, [name the title of the book], a chapter in the book sounds like Jesus' strategy for the church in Acts 1:8. The author, [name the author] said that to be successful in real estate sales a salesman needs to *farm* his community. That means he needs to identify his area, then go door-to-door and meet every homeowner. Realize that sooner or later every property will sell. When the owner thinks "sell," we want them to think our company and you as an agent.

If you are going to contact them only once, do not do it. You must meet them personally, then write them a note. Later, give them a phone call. Later, go back and leave a note on the door. Send them a mail-out. When they think sell, they will call on you and our company.

Corporate America has learned the principles Jesus gave us in Acts 1:8. They do work! Why can't churches understand and practice Jesus' strategy? If I were in a secular corporation, I would use Jesus' strategy for financial profit. What? Yes! These principles are God-given, human, organizational, and motivational principles. People have to know about the Gospel and about your church. The principles work! Why don't we believe God and use them?

Dr. Darrell W. Robinson

What are the positive results of geographic saturation?

Geographic saturation has multi-faceted positive results and advantages. It accomplishes some critically-needed community relationships for the church and for the witness of our Lord.

1. *It creates a climate for evangelism and a God-consciousness in the church's community.* As we saturate the Jerusalem of our church periodically, people will begin to think, *God, I need God!* In our community a fourteen-year-old boy, Herman, came to our church office and spoke to my secretary, Jean. I was out of the office that afternoon. Herman said, "I was at the grocery store and someone gave me this tract about Jesus and his coming again. I realized that I need him. Jean began to share Christ with him. He said that he had gone to three churches and could not find anyone. Though his father had forbidden him to go across the busy street to get to our church, he was so under conviction that he came anyway. Jean led Herman to Christ! They rejoiced!

   That evening, I went to Herman's home. As we visited, his father Joe said, "Since Herman did his disappearing act, I know I need Jesus." I thought he was speaking about Herman's disappearance from home and going to our church across the busy streets. That was not it.

   Joe said, "Herman did the disappearing act. He came back from your church and said, 'Dad, you, Mom, and I are going to be sitting here and suddenly, *poof!* Mom and I will be gone and you will be left sitting here by yourself! Jesus is coming to take us and leave you behind!' Pastor, I need Christ." Joe prayed and received Christ. The family came to church, were baptized, and continued to follow Christ.

   This is an example of a God-consciousness in a community that resulted in a family's coming to Christ.

2. *Saturation evangelism, especially witnessing door-to door has immediate results.* You will knock on the doors of some people who are ready to receive Christ. As the plan of salvation is shared with them, they will pray and receive Christ. Our church did a Sunday afternoon Bible distribution. One of our teams knocked

70

on the door of Jim and Nancy. The Holy Spirit was working in their lives. They received the marked New Testament gratefully and told the team that they were interested in church, but had no church home. The team went through the marked verses in Romans and asked them if they would like to pray and receive Christ. They prayed. Then they came with the team to church and confessed Christ.

Jim and Nancy became soulwinners and leaders in the church.

The story behind Bible distribution in our town was miraculous. As their pastor, I shared with our people in the church that I believed God wanted us to take a copy of a marked New Testament to every home in our Jerusalem. There were fifty-two thousand homes, including apartments, in the area. One of our men worked for a home builder. He told the owner. The owner met with me and said, "I will purchase every marked New Testament you can give out."

We did a saturation witness survey and went to every home and apartment in the area. Many accepted Christ and many more came to Christ and the church. The great truth God showed us was that "What God desires us to do, he will provide for us to do!" God finances his initiatives!

,We have helped churches perform saturation witness surveys in every region in America. We did it in connection with Schools of Evangelism and Crossover, which I was instrumental in starting when I was vice president for evangelism at the Southern Baptist Home Mission Board. The statistics are that when the Gospel was presented six times, one person prayed and received Christ. Some of the diverse places where it was done were: New Jersey, Philadelphia, Greensborough, Albuquerque, Denver, Chicago, Kansas City, Oklahoma City, New Orleans, Orlando, Ft. Lauderdale, Houston, Dallas, Los Angeles, San Jose, Portland, Honolulu, Santa Fe, and Las Vegas, along with other smaller places.

3. *Prospects for the witness of the church are discovered.* In many homes are people who do not know Christ. We discover them through the saturation witness survey. We get their names, addresses, and phone numbers and keep a record in the church

71

in order to follow up. In our church, we had names and information on thousands of prospects. We stayed in touch with them and followed-up in witness periodically. The result was that there were many first-time visits to the church and every Sunday people confessed Christ who had been reached through the follow up by our members. Saturation evangelism does work!

4. *Saturation evangelism gives the opportunity for church members to be involved in the greatest joy a Christian can experience— witnessing for Christ and leading people to him.* If only the pastor and staff have this joy, we are cheating our people out of God's great blessing.

5. *Saturation evangelism can result in the church experiencing revival.* The Holy Spirit moves mightily as a church becomes a witnessing body of Christ. Churches today that train and equip every member to share Jesus and lead people to Christ are experiencing revival.

Develop a prospect discovery and record system.

For geographic saturation to have maximum effectiveness, a planned organizational system needs to be developed and implemented to discover prospects and to keep accurate records on them. Otherwise, they may be overlooked or neglected and not be reached for Christ.

Organize a discovery system—prepare the church to discover every prospect in its Jerusalem.

For a church to continue to reach the lost and experience evangelistic growth, it needs to have a wealth of names of people who need Christ and the church in its outreach file. Discovering them must be both an ongoing process and periodic extensive discovery projects.

1. *Develop church-wide sensitivity to the lost and non-churched.* The pastor should take the lead in creating such a spirit in the church. People do what leaders do!

   • By preaching on such subjects as "what it means to be lost" and challenge the church to reach every lost person.

- By modeling sensitivity to lost people by being personally involved in reaching them for Christ and taking members with him to visit with them.

- By personally discovering and identifying people who need Christ and the church and asking members who have something in common with them to visit them.

- By recording their names and information into the outreach file.

2. *Define what you mean by a "prospect."* Teach the church that a prospect is any person who does not personally know Jesus Christ or is not an active member in any church. These are "prospects" for our church's witness and ministry. It is our purpose to continue to share Christ and minister to them until the person is saved and actively involved in the life of a church, moves away, or dies.

3. *Define your church's geographical area or areas of primary responsibility for witness.* The pastor leads the church in defining the geographic area or areas for which it will accept primary responsibility to pray and to saturate periodically with the gospel, discover every prospect, and continue to minister and witness to each prospect.

4. *Make the most of your outreach (prospect) file.* Set up an outreach prospect file and develop a system of assignment that guarantees that every prospect will receive a periodic witnessing contact.

The pastor and outreach leader should read through the names in the file and pray for each from time to time. An outreach secretary should be given the responsibility for keeping the file updated (recording visits made and results) and for preparing prospect assignments each week for visitation. The outreach prospect file should include:
1. A method of identifying prospective families
2. A method of identifying individual prospects
3. A method of identifying every lost prospect
4 A method of identifying every non-churched prospect

5. *Develop a prospect mentality.* This should include the determination to:
   - Discover and have in the outreach prospect file the name and information needed on every prospect in the church's Jerusalem (geographic area and areas of influence).
   - Place the name of every church guest who is a prospect in the file and follow up on that person.
   - Lead members to submit prospect names from their circle of acquaintances. Some churches use a "who-do" card. That is who-do-you-know who need Christ. The pastor asks members to take five minutes at the Sunday morning worship service to list the name and address, if they know it and submit it for prayer and outreach visitation. This is a good way to find prospects.

Select a Discovery Task Force to Develop the Discovery System

1. Enlist and train the task force. They should be people who have a passion to reach the lost for Christ. They should also be gifted in organization and administration. They are to assist the pastor in leading the church to find every lost and non-churched person in the church's Jerusalem.

2. Schedule a time for a task force member to meet with new members in their homes. Congratulate each new member on their decision for Christ. Ask them if they have family members and friends who need Christ. Each new member has a "circle of influence" and acquaintance of people who need a witness for Christ.

3. Use the forms at the end of Chapter 3 of *People Sharing Jesus* for new members to fill in the names of family members, friends, contacts in the marketplace, and contacts in the daily traffic patterns who need Christ. Ask them to fill in the names while you are there. Pray with them for their family and friends. Ask if they would consider going to visit them and sharing what has happened in their lives when they received Christ. Offer to go with them or get another member of the

church to go with them. Get a copy of their list to add to the church's prospect file.

4. Share with the church the biblical principles of praying for the lost. "Therefore I exhort first of all that supplications, prayers, intercessions, and giving of thanks be made for all men, for kings and all who are in authority, that we may lead a quiet and peaceable life in all godliness and reverence. For this is good and acceptable in the sight of God our Savior, who desires all men to be saved and to come to the knowledge of the truth" (1 Timothy 2:1-4 NKJV). We need to pray for the lost. God wants all men to be saved. Lead the church members to pray for the lost. Especially involve new members in praying for their lost family members and friends.

5. When new believers are baptized, send a formal invitation to their families, friends, and acquaintances to attend the baptism and a reception for the new member. Follow up with visits to these. We can find many new prospects through our new members.

6. Lost people may be found through involvement with people in their daily lives and activities such as weddings, funerals, school activities, ball games, businesses, and stores. Members should submit names of these people to the church office to be placed in the prospect file and followed up.

Consider Other Methods of Prospect Discovery and Identification

Use every possible means to discover the people in your area of ministry and witness and get the information into your outreach prospect file. Follow up periodically.

1. Secure the name and information on every guest of the church's worship services and other meetings. Use a guest card, guest registration, and members getting acquainted and reporting information. Follow up with a visit in their home. Record their information in the outreach prospect file.

2. The pastor and members develop prospect sensitivity in their traffic patterns of life (keep a notepad to record information as they meet people who need Christ).

3. Conduct periodic *inside* prospect discovery.
   - Search through the Sunday school records to identify lost Sunday school members.
   - Periodically examine the church membership roll to identify lost relatives of members.
   - From time-to-time, lead the Sunday school classes to fill out the "who-do" cards mentioned above.

4. Periodically conduct a door-to-door saturation witness/survey to lead people to Christ and discover prospects. Get acquainted with every resident. Through conversation at the door, determine whether or not they are prospects. A conversation guide or religious opinion poll may be used. Go as far as possible in sharing Christ at the door. Some will be ready to be saved at the first contact. Leave a Gospel tract and information about the church or a church event.

5. Do a telephone survey of your area. Train callers for a prospect discovery conversation. Call every number in the designated area. You may use a city directory or telephone directory.

6. Use direct mail. Direct mail may be used for periodic contact to cultivate all prospects. "Return requested" stamped on the envelopes should be used to determine if prospects have moved. A visit should be made to the new resident at the address as quickly as possible.

7. Use special evangelistic events. Periodic and varied events should be conducted to attract prospects. Secure the names of all who attend. A trained telephone task force should call every guest. A follow-up phone call and visit should be made to every prospect.

8. Interview every new member to determine who they know who needs Christ and join them in seeking to reach them for Christ. (See earlier explanation of a discovery task force.)

Geographic saturation works synergistically with the other biblical techniques to enhance the evangelistic outreach of a church. Along with public proclamation, caring ministry, and event attraction, it will combine to reach many more for Christ than a single technique approach. The church that implements geographic saturation will find that more people will come to the worship services for public proclamation, even people you didn't personally reach. It will be an opportunity to reach them.

Dick Jones was not home when one of our members stopped by his home in our witness/survey Bible distribution. The member shared with Dick's brother and left a marked New Testament that had our church's information on the back cover. He laid the New Testament on the table where Dick saw it and picked it up. Dick read it and came to our church. He confessed his faith and was baptized. Today Dick is a fine pastor of a church.

Many more will attend the event attraction events. You will also discover people who have needs that your church can meet through your caring ministry. God will bless the church's entire evangelistic ministry synergistically through geographic saturation.

The fifth of the evangelistic techniques found in the Book of Acts is personal presentation of the Gospel of Christ through personal witnessing. As church members are trained and equipped to share Jesus in the power of the Holy Spirit, the power of the church to reach the lost for Christ is enhanced to an even greater extent. We will consider personal presentation in Chapter Seven.

CHAPTER SEVEN
Personal Presentation

Acts 1:8; Matthew 28:18-20; Acts 8:26-39

"But you will receive power when the Holy Spirit has come upon you; and YOU WILL BE MY WITNESSES [the *you* is plural—it means all of you] in Jerusalem, in all Judea and Samaria, and to the ends of the earth" (Acts 1:8 HCSB, with my words in brackets).

"Then Jesus came near and said to them, 'All authority has been given to Me in heaven and on earth. Go, therefore, and make disciples of all the nations, baptizing them in the name of the Father and of the Son and of the Holy Spirit, teaching them to observe everything I have commanded you; and remember, I am with you always, to the end of the age'" (Matthew 28:18-20 HCSB).

Personal Presentation of the Gospel is Foundational in Reaching the Lost

For the first four techniques to result in maximum fruitfulness of reaching people, the fifth technique is absolutely necessary. People come to Christ one by one. Many must be personally guided through the conversion experience by a caring believer. This is what happened with the Ethiopian eunuch who was guided through the conversion experience by Phillip in the desert. If personal presentation through witnessing and soulwinning is neglected, though a church may implement the first four techniques, it will result in fewer people being saved and baptized.

Personal presentation is the equipping of members to be spiritually sensitive and intentional in sharing of the claims of Christ with an individual so that he or she can understand and respond to his claims on his or her life. It involves a caring believer in guiding a lost person through the conversion experience under the leadership of the Holy Spirit.

Personally sharing the Gospel is wonderfully illustrated in the story of Philip and the Ethiopian eunuch in Acts 8. Philip had been one of those who was "scattered from Jerusalem at the stoning of Stephen and went everywhere evangelizing." Philip went to Samaria. God used him to reach many. A mighty revival broke out. Then, an angel of the Lord spoke to him and told him to go down to the desert of Gaza.

Who was in the desert? No one! But, Philip was obedient and went. It just so happened that he crossed the path of a caravan from Ethiopia … or, did it just happen? No! It was not a coincidence—it was a God incident, a divine appointment! God gives divine appointments to his people every day. Like Philip, we need to be sensitive to the Holy Spirit and to the person who needs to be reached. When we are insensitive, the divine appointment passes without our realizing it. We need to pray daily that we will be sensitive to the Holy Spirit and to the people we meet so we will recognize the divine appointments that God gives us. God gives us divine appointments almost every day!

The Ethiopian was the treasurer of Queen Candace. He was reading from the Book of Isaiah, particularly from the Messianic passage in Isaiah 53:7-8. The Holy Spirit said to Philip, "Go and join that chariot" (Acts 8:29 HCSB). Philip ran to him and saw him reading from the book of Isaiah.

This was intentional witnessing! If we are to be effective in personal presentation, we must be intentional. Philip began to converse with the Ethiopian in a nonthreatening way. He simply asked, "Do you understand what you're reading?" (Acts 8:30 HCSB) Effective witnessing involves nonthreatening conversation that leads to a presentation of Christ and the Gospel.

The Ethiopian said, "How can I, unless someone guides me?" (Acts 8:31 HCSB) Do you know why many in your community are not being saved? It is because **nobody asks them**! One evening I made a quick hospital visit on my way to another meeting. I wanted to cultivate Bill, who was lost. He was ill. I visited for about three minutes and had prayer. As I was praying, the Holy Spirit spoke to my heart and impressed me that I had never asked him to receive Christ. Immediately, I stopped the prayer and said, "Bill, I want to apologize to you. We have talked several times, but I have never asked you to receive Christ. I want to ask you now to pray with me and receive Christ." He prayed and received Christ with joy. He had not been saved because nobody had asked him. Do you know why many in your church's Jerusalem are not being saved? Nobody asks them! Let's simply ask people to come to Christ. Many will!

Philip explained the good news of Christ from Isaiah 53. He tenderly guided the Ethiopian through the conversion experience. The Ethiopian believed and requested baptism. Tradition says that he went back to Ethiopia and started the great Ethiopian church that continues to this day in that country.

Multitudes can be reached for Christ as believers are equipped for soulwinning. It should be the goal of every pastor to inspire and equip every member to lead people to Christ and to guide them tenderly through the conversion experience and into the life of the church. For maximum effectiveness and fruitfulness in reaching its community for Christ, a church should incorporate all of the five techniques of balanced evangelism.

The Ethiopian incident is a great lesson on what God uses to bring the lost to Christ. Three elements were involved. God uses an unbeatable team of three.

God's Unbeatable Team to Reach the Lost

First: The Word of God! Philip guided the Ethiopian through Isaiah 53.

The Word of God Builds Faith

God promised, "Faith comes from what is heard, and what is heard comes through the message about Christ" (Romans 10:17 HCSB). It is the Word of God that instills faith in the human heart. It is like seed that sprouts, grows, and produces the fruit of faith in Christ.

The Word of God is Power to Save

"I am not ashamed of the gospel, for it is God's power for salvation" (Romans 1:16 HCSB). The Gospel of Christ is the power that converts people to Christ. We must share the Gospel with every person in obedience to Christ and his commission.

Many in our day have all but lost confidence in the power of the Gospel. They think that we must depend on cultural relevancy, slick presentations, or psychological manipulation. But the Gospel of Christ has innately within it the mighty power of God.

In Edinburgh, Scotland, I was leading a Total Church Life Seminar at the University of Edinburgh. The event was The International Conference on Preaching. In setting up for my seminar, I spoke to George, a university official.

I conversed with him and asked, "George, may I ask you a question? Have you come to know Jesus Christ in a personal way or would you say you are still in the process?"

George said, "No, I am an atheist!"

"May I share with you something that has been very meaningful to me? It is a little booklet called *Eternal Life*."

"Sure," George said. We continued and went through the booklet.

When we came to the page of the prayer, I asked, "George, after reading the passages from the Bible, I want to ask you, will you believe in God and in his son, Jesus Christ now?"

George waited, and then said, "Yes, I will!" I led him to pray and receive Christ as Savior and Lord.

Then I asked him, "Who do you know who you want to share what has happened to you?"

He said, "My wife. She will be excited about it."

As we went down the hall to my specified room, we met some other conference leaders. I asked George to share with them what had happened to him. He said, "I just prayed and received Jesus Christ in my life."

This is the power of the Gospel!

Dusk was falling as Kathy and I walked from the University of Edinburgh to our hotel. Along with Jeff Harvel, a young evangelist friend, we walked past an old church building that had been closed. In front of it was a woman surrounded by a group of people. She had props about witches and a tour to the witches. She was dressed in a black robe and hood. Her face was painted black, grey, and white. She was shouting, "Come with me to the witches! Come with me to the witches!"

I stopped for a moment. Kathy said, "Come on. Let's go to the hotel. I am cold." I started to go on with her.

Then, the Holy Spirit reprimanded me. "You hypocrite, this woman was promoting the witches and you said nothing for Jesus."

"Kathy," I said, "I want to go back and see what this is all about."

She said, "I am cold, I am going on to the hotel."

Jeff and I went back and listened at the edge of the crowd. Then, something unusual happened to me. Usually, I am reserved and stand back and listen. At this moment I found myself putting my hand to my mouth and shouting, "Jesus is Lord! Jesus is Lord! Satan has no authority over you except what you grant him!"

One man loudly said, "Amen!"

Another said, "That's right!"

A young man walked up and said, "This man is right! There is nothing to this!"

I turned to him and said, "This is great! I am glad to meet another believer!"

"Believer," he responded, "I am an atheist!"

"Tell me about yourself, where are you from?"

He answered, "I am from Australia. Where are you from, Canada? Or, are you from the US?"

"I am from the US. What brought you all the way to Edinburgh?"

He explained, "I am an engineer and we are having a conference for engineers."

"Wait a minute. I am having a difficult time computing what you have told me. You are an engineer and an atheist! How is that possible? Engineers do everything you do based on absolutes. Absolute design! Absolute plan! For there to be a design, there must be a designer. For there to be a plan, there must be a planner."

He was surprised, "I never thought of that."

"Could I share with you briefly about that?" Then I shared the Gospel of Christ and asked him if at that moment he would believe in

God and that his son, Jesus Christ, gave his life on the cross for him and his salvation?

The young engineer from Australia took my hand and said, "Yes! I will believe in him now!"

This is indeed the power of the Gospel!

The Word of God is the sword of the Spirit. "… and the sword of the Spirit, which is the Word of God" (Ephesians 6:17 HCSB).

"For the Word of God is living and effective, and sharper than any two-edged sword, penetrating as far as to divide soul, spirit, joints, and marrow; it is a judge of the ideas and thoughts of the heart" (Hebrews 4:12 HCSB). What a mighty power is intrinsic in the Word of God! It pierces in more deeply than human counsel can reach. It probes into the spirit level of a human life where change is made. As change comes into the spirit level of a life, the change will permeate the entire life. The birth of the Spirit takes place at this level. Human counsel, if it is good counsel, can affect a person at the "soul" level of life. It can affect the mind to guide thinking; the emotion to help a person maintain control and develop positive emotions; and the will to help a person in decision making. But, human counsel cannot reach into the spirit level of a life. Only the Word of God can do this and change the person.

The Word of God "judges the ideas and thoughts of the heart" so that a person has revealed to himself/herself the truth about the thoughts of the heart. Not only are the thoughts revealed, but the intentions that produce the thoughts. As I have preached the Word, I have had people say, "Pastor, you might as well to have called my name in this sermon." Actually, I would not have realized that they were present. I simply preached the Word and it "judges the ideas and thoughts of the heart."

The Word of God Crushes Hard Hearts and Melts Icy Hearts

"Is not My word like a fire," said the Lord, "and like a sledgehammer that pulverizes rock?" (Jeremiah 23:29 HCSB) God's Word is like a fire that can melt the coldest heart. It is like a hammer that can break the hard and stony heart.

Second: The Work of the Spirit! The Holy Spirit led Philip to the Ethiopian.

The Holy Spirit was given for witness to Christ. He leads and empowers each believer. As we witness, Holy Spirit power flows (Acts 1:8).

The Holy Spirit Convicts the Lost

The Holy Spirit uses the Word of God as his sword to pierce the heart and mind of the lost and bring conviction (Ephesians 6:17; John 16:8-11).

He convicts "of sin, because they do not believe in Me" (vs. 9). When we witness, we cannot convict of sin. If we try, the person to whom we are witnessing will probably become defensive. This job belongs to the Holy Spirit.

He convicts "of righteousness, because I go to my Father and you see Me no more" (vs. 10). Jesus is righteous, but he is not physically present. The Holy Spirit reveals and convinces the human heart of Jesus and his righteousness.

He convicts "of judgment, because the ruler of this world is judged" (vs. 11). The Holy Spirit reveals and convinces the human heart that Satan has been judged and condemned and that if they follow him rather than Jesus, they are also judged and condemned. People are often convicted and shaken as they realize the judgment they face.

The Holy Spirit draws lost people to Christ. "No one can come to Me unless the Father who sent Me draws him, and I will raise him up at the last day" (John 6:44 HCSB). God, through the Holy Spirit, draws people to Jesus. I have witnessed to many who rejected Christ, but later they accepted Christ because the Holy Spirit used the "seed of the Word" and nurtured the Word of God in their hearts to draw them to Christ.

The Holy Spirit Works in the Lives of Believers to Lead the Lost to Christ

He gives the believer the words to say. "Don't worry about how you should defend yourselves or what you should say. For the Holy Spirit will teach you at that very hour what must be said" (Luke 12:11b-12). Some Christians use the excuse for not witnessing that they are afraid they won't know what to say. We should simply say what we know! We do know Jesus and what he has done in our lives. Simply say it! If we do not know what to say, we can study the scriptures and participate in witness training and learn what to say. However, we will never learn everything needed to lead someone to Christ. It is a Holy Spirit work. We need to start doing it.

How do you learn to swim? You may read a book or go to a swimming class and study the strokes and how to breathe in the water. But with that approach you will never learn to swim. How do you learn to swim? You simply dive in! That is true with soulwinning. You simply dive in and do it. Rely on God's promise that the Holy Spirit will put his words in our mouths. He will!

It was Christmastime. I went back to West Texas to visit my mom. It was very cold. One day she asked me to do something for her. I said, "Sure, what do you want me to do?"

She said, "I want you to visit Omar. He has been going with Wilma, your cousin, to Salem Church. He is in Clyde's Sunday school class and has been asking some questions. I think you could answer them."

"Sure, I'll go," I said, but truthfully I really did not want to. What will I say? Omar was a retired Air Force person, divorced, claimed to be an atheist. Wilma's husband died and the two married. That afternoon I drove to the edge of town where they lived. There was a butane gas truck delivering gas to their tank. Omar was talking to the driver. I passed on by and decided to go down the road and come back in a few minutes. "If the gas truck is gone, I will stop," I thought.

It was gone and I stopped. I knocked on the door not knowing what I would say. They invited me in and we visited and caught up on what had been happening in our lives. I used the FIRM acronym in visiting. I thought, "How would I get started in sharing Christ?" I decided to take the direct approach. I said, "Omar, let me tell you why I am here. Mother asked me to visit with you. She said you have been going with Wilma to Salem and you have been asking questions that Clyde, your teacher, can't answer. I don't know if I can answer them or not, but I will try."

Omar said, "I do have a question. Why do bad things happen to good people?"

Now, I have three doctoral degrees, but can you guess what I told him? I simply said, "Omar, I don't know!" I did know all the classical answers and had studied this very question in philosophy and theology, but here was a question that did not need to be answered. Something we need to practice is to be honest. If we do not know the answer to a question, don't make something up. Just say you do not know, but that you will search for the answer and talk again.

This time I said, "Omar, I know that bad things have happened to both of us. You had a divorce, your wife left you. What a sorrow that was. My first wife, Betty, died just as we were beginning in our ministry. The bottom dropped out. I do not understand why these things happened. But, I don't have to understand because I know Jesus and believe Romans 8:28, "All things work together for good to those who love God, to those who are the called according to His purpose." I believe that God wants to give us his highest and best in our lives. He wants us to know him. "Have you come to know him in a personal way or are you still in the process?"

"I am in the process," Omar said.

"Then, you have thought about it?" I asked.

"Yes, I have thought about it."

"May I show you how you can receive Christ and know him?" I asked.

"Sure!" I shared the Gospel with Omar and thought he would immediately pray and receive Christ, but he refused.

I asked, "Why will you not receive him, Omar?"

Omar said, "I just don't have the feeling!"

The Holy Spirit moved my heart and put his words in my mouth. I said, "Omar, what kind of feeling do you think you need to have?"

He responded, "I don't know."

I asked, "May I tell you?"

"Sure!"

"Omar, you need to feel like you are a sinner and you are sorry for it. You need to feel like Christ died for your sins and you are grateful for it. You need to feel like God wants to save you and you want him to do it."

Then, very moved by the Spirit, Omar said, "I feel like that!"

Omar prayed with me and received Christ. He and Wilma were filled with joy. Omar went to church on Sunday and Omar confessed Christ and was baptized. He became the handyman at the church.

He even uses our mess-ups. He would have to, since all of us mess up. Between the worst and the best of us, there is not enough difference to make any difference. To use any of us, he would have to use us in spite of us. The Holy Spirit is the soulwinner, but he uses us in the process. Some Christians use as the reason that they do not witness that they fear that they may mess up. But he can even use our mess-ups. Actually, non-believers may relate to us better when they see our humanness. We can apologize for our failures and point them to the fact that we are not presenting ourselves as above failure. We can tell them that we are sharing with them about Jesus who never fails.

A humorous example is what happened to my pastor friend, James. James tells it like this. On his way home, he stopped by the grocery store. There he met a member named Sue. Sue told him that she was having difficulty with her husband and might need to call the pastor for him to come to their home.

That night at about 1:00 AM, James phone rang. The voice said, "Hello Pastor, this is Sue. Things are not good here. Could you come to our home?" James got up and went to the home of Sue whom he had spoken at the store. He knocked on the door. Sue came to the door in her nightgown and robe. Her husband was sitting in his big chair watching the late show.

It was late, James got right into his witness. He said, "Friend, you have not been giving spiritual leadership to your family. You need to repent, get right with God, and receive Jesus Christ as your Savior and Lord! Let's get on our knees and pray."

The husband fell on his knees and prayed and received Christ. The next Sunday, Sue and her husband came forward and he confessed Christ.

Now for the surprising and humorous part. Down the aisle came the other Sue and her husband. She said, "Pastor, when you did not come to our house when I called, I talked to my husband about Jesus myself. He received Christ and has come with me today to confess Christ and join the church."

What a story about how God used James' mess up. Can you imagine the shock of the first of the two Sues when the pastor knocked on the door after 1:00 AM? The Holy Spirit is mighty and wonderful in his work to bring people to Christ.

He leads the believer so that divine appointments happen. "For as many as are led by the Spirit of God, these are the sons of God" (Romans

8:14 NKJV). Philip witnessing to the Ethiopian in the desert is a great example.

It was on a Wednesday. I was supposed to preach at a special evangelism meeting of First Baptist Church in Dallas, Texas. I went early to visit with the Texas evangelism director in the Baptist Building in Dallas. After the visit, I went into the restroom to freshen up. I was washing my face and realized that a man was in another corner cleaning the restroom. The Spirit impressed me to witness to the man. Do you ever get an impression like that? If you do, you had better do it. The devil does not give those impressions. It was the Holy Spirit.

But, in my mind I argued. "We are in the restroom!"

Again, the impression came, "Witness to him."

Again, I hesitated, "He is in the Baptist Building. The employees here witness all the time. They have witnessed to him."

Again, the impression came, "Witness to him." I thought of another excuse, "I am due soon to be at First Baptist. If I witness to him, I will be late!"

Then, the Holy Spirit gave another impression. I thought, "You may be the last Christian to cross his path before he stands before God. Witness to him!" With that I turned and did not even dry my face.

I said, "Friend, may I ask you a question?"

"Sure."

"Are you a saved man?" I did not know if he knew what saved meant. If he did not, I would explain it to him. Please understand that I am sharing about how to share Christ in a natural and nonthreatening way through using dialogue and a conversation guide, FIRM. However, when the Holy Spirit leads you, just do it. I took the very direct approach.

The man replied, "No sir, but I would surely like to be." In three or four minutes, he prayed and received Christ and said he would go to church in his neighborhood and confess Christ and ask the pastor to help him grow in Christ. The Holy Spirit had given me a divine appointment in the restroom in the Baptist Building in Texas. In spite of my resistance, he used me to guide a man he was drawing to Christ through the conversion experience.

Third: The Witnessing Believer! Philip was the witnessing believer. Paul, with his passion for people, was a witnessing believer (Roman

9:1-3). If every Christian is sensitive to the Holy Spirit and to the people they meet and is committed to share Christ, many will be saved and follow Christ.

This is the unbeatable team of three that God uses to reach people for Christ. It was true in the New Testament times and it is true today. This gives great confidence for us to witness for Christ. It is God who does it and we simply get in on what God is doing! What an encouraging truth! We cannot bring people to Christ. We simply share the Word of God and the Holy Spirit does the work of drawing them to Christ. We are available to guide them through the conversion experience as the Holy Spirit draws them.

One Sunday morning, I had preached the Gospel as clearly and fervently as I knew how. I had explained how to pray and receive Christ and had even asked those who were lost to repeat a prayer of repentance and faith to receive Christ. After the message, I stood at the door and greeted the people. Jeri, our travel agent who had been led to Christ on the telephone by my secretary, Jean, while she was scheduling my travel, had brought her fiancée, Mark, with her. Jeri introduced Mark to me and said that they wanted to visit with me. I asked them to wait a few minutes until I had greeted the people and we would visit.

Mark said that he was interested in the church. I asked if anyone had ever explained to him how he could receive Christ. Mark said, "No! No one ever has."

That was interesting! I had just explained the Gospel and given him the prayer to pray to receive Christ. Mark did not hear! The lost do not understand. These things are spiritually understood! (1 Corinthians 2:14-15) I quietly shared the plan of salvation and led him to pray. I did as Philip did with the Ethiopian! The Holy Spirit was drawing him. All I did was simply to guide him through the conversion experience.

This is like an obstetrician. The obstetrician does not make the baby nor have the baby. All the obstetrician does is to "guide a woman through the delivery." All I did with Mark was to guide him through the conversion experience. Every believer can learn to cooperate with the Holy Spirit and lead those who need Jesus through the conversion experience.

The Priority of Personal Witnessing

It is what God wants! God wants all men to be saved!

"This is good and it pleases God our Savior, who wants everyone to be saved and to come to the knowledge of the truth" (1 Timothy

2:3-4 HCSB). God is at work to get the Gospel to every person. He uses people to do it—people like us!

God loves every person! "For God so loved the world in this way; He gave His One and Only Son, so that everyone who believes in Him will not perish but have eternal life" (John 3:16 HCSB).

You will never look into the face of a person that God does not love and for whom Christ did not die. Every one of them is a treasure to God. God loves every person and Christ died on the cross for each one. For many years I jogged every morning wherever I might have been. In some of the great cities of our world, I have stepped over the bodies of people on the streets and wondered if they were dead or alive. I would ask myself, "Is there any hope for him?" Yes, there is hope as long as he is alive. He is a treasure to God! God has unlimited potential for this life as he comes to Christ.

Bob Smith is a great illustration of this truth. I was visiting door-to-door in a western suburb of Chicago and met Bob. I asked him if he knew Jesus Christ as his savior and Lord. Bob gave me his testimony that for twenty years he was a wino on the streets of Chicago. Often, he would wake up from a stupor in a gutter on the street. One cold, winter morning he awakened, about to freeze. He had put cardboard in his shoes and stuffed newspapers in his coat. He was hungry and went into a mission center for a bowl of soup. He heard them talk about Jesus. A few days later he went to another mission center for soup. That day he left changed. He had received Jesus Christ.

Bob found a little job, got a room, bought some clothes, and got a better job. He contacted his wife, from whom he had been separated for twenty years. They got back together and now live in a little white bungalow in western Chicago. I asked, "Bob, have you been baptized and do you have a church?"

He answered, "No, do I need to be baptized?" I explained baptism to him. That night he and his wife came to church and confessed Christ as Savior and Lord. He was baptized and became an active member of the church. God used him to reach others for Christ

While Bob was lying in the gutter, there was hope. He was a treasure to God with unlimited potential for his Lord! Thank God, someone shared Christ with him.

Every person is a treasure to God!

None are so far gone that God cannot deal with them. God "is able to do above and beyond all that we ask or think—according to the power that works in you—to Him be glory in the church and in Christ Jesus to all generations, forever and forever" (Ephesians 3:20-21 HCSB). One of those who seemed too far gone for God to reach was Carl. He wore a black jacket and heavy boots and rode a motorcycle. Though he was on drugs, he worked at a petroleum plant. Carl contracted hepatitis, possibly from a bad needle while taking drugs. He was deathly sick, but a compassionate Christian man moved into Carl's house and nurtured him through his illness. By the time he was on his feet again, Carl was converted.

The first time I saw Carl was when he came forward to confess Christ in our church. He was a big, big guy with his hair down to his belt in the back and his beard down to his belt in his front. He was quite a spectacle to behold. Our members accepted him and reached out to him. I got him into a men's Bible study group that met in a restaurant at 6:30 AM on Tuesdays. We kept it simple. In the group were contractors, lawyers, plant workers, doctors, and dentists. Our procedure was to use a Christian Life New Testament with study outlines. At each meeting someone would read a scripture and a point in the outline. Then, we would open it for questions and discussion. The guys delighted in putting me on the spot with their questions. I enjoyed it, too. One Tuesday I had to be away. I asked one of our staff to cover for me. When I returned, my associate said, "Pastor, I will do whatever you ask me to do, but, please, don't ask me to meet with the 'Wild Bunch' again!" It was quite an unorthodox group.

Carl participated and one day told me that he thought he could what I did in leading a group at his plant in Bible studies. He asked me to give him some of the marked New Testaments to give out at the plant. He tried to give them to workers, but none would take them. Not to be defeated, Carl placed them on the break room table. Soon they were gone and he would replace them with another box of marked New Testaments. He got an appointment with his boss and asked to have a Bible study time at lunch one day each week.

His boss remarked, "Carl, you have been in here for every kind of thing, now this. What few Christians I have at this plant, I am not going to turn them over to you for you to ruin them." But, Carl continued to persist in getting a Bible study started. Finally, he got approval. Three or four came the first week and, then, a few more. Carl came up with an idea to get a crowd. He called Big George! You know him, George Foreman, the world champion prize fighter! George had been saved and had a good testimony. He said, "Yes, I will come and give my testimony at your Bible study."

More than three hundred people came to hear George's testimony. Several accepted Christ. Carl's Bible study grew. The end result was that the plant management began to videotape the Bible studies and send them to others of their plants as "an example of morale building" in a plant. God was using a man who had been a "hopeless reject" in the eyes of man, but to God he was a treasure with unlimited potential.

A few months, later Carl went with an Evangelism Team and me to Sao Paulo, Brazil. We were told not to go on the streets alone because of the extreme danger. Carl ignored the instruction and went alone down the street to a newspaper stand. As he was making a purchase, a man elbowed him, grabbed his wallet and passport, and ran. Carl raced after him. Someone tripped the man and Carl tackled him and rolled him into the gutter. The man had a knife which Carl took from him. He sat on top of the man, took out of his pocket a leaflet with his testimony in Portuguese and a presentation of the Gospel on it. Carl stumbled through reading it to the man while he held him down with his other hand. Carl was a big, tough guy who was streetwise.

On Sunday, Carl went alone by taxi to preach at a church. On the way he led the taxi driver to Christ. He was so excited that he left his briefcase with his passport and credit cards in the taxi. When he returned to the hotel, he was dismayed. He thought that he would never see his briefcase again. But he was surprised the next morning when the taxi driver showed up at the hotel with his briefcase and nothing inside had been touched. The driver, would you believe, brought Carl a gift and thanked him for leading him to Christ. God used this big, passionate guy in Brazil to lead people to Christ! God wants to save every person and he works through every means to accomplish what he desires! Carl was a treasure to God!

God wants us to use every Christian in witness for Christ! ACTS 1:8

Years ago, in 1956, Dr. C. E. Matthews wrote *The Southern Baptist Program of Evangelism.* In it he laid out the plan to encourage a climate for evangelism in every church and to train every member to witness. His theme was "Witnessing—Every Christian's Job!" Through this approach Southern Baptist Churches all over the nation experienced revival and reached multitudes for Christ. This truth did not begin with C. E. Matthews. It began with Jesus in his great commission!

With certainty in the first century Jesus called every Christian to witness. Jesus has not changed. The Bible has not changed. Witnessing is still every Christian's job.

To whom are we to witness?

We are to witness to our family and friends. These are often the most difficult people to whom we can witness. Why?

First, we think we know them. They never talk about Christ and their need of him. Their lifestyle may not show any evidence of a spiritual concern. The focus of their lives may be on making money, having pleasure, or their work. Very easily we can withdraw and lay aside our purpose of sharing Christ with them concluding that they would not listen anyway!

One day at noon I was making visits through our community. It was a rural area. We had identified our Jerusalem on a map. We had gone to every home except one. It was a home on a ranch that was difficult to reach. Besides this, the church people said that these people were Mormons. We did not go there. I didn't know anything about Mormons. But, on this day I felt the Lord leading me to go to their home. The man, Horace, was filling his tractor with gasoline. I introduced myself. He said, "Yes, I know who you are. My wife, Jewell, will want to talk to you." We went inside and his wife did want to talk about Christ. Shortly, she received Jesus and Horace recommitted his life to Christ! They came to church, were baptized, and became faithful members and leaders. Later, I found that they had attended a Mormon church with a relative one time. The church people thought they knew them! But, in reality, they did not know them. They needed Jesus and we were avoiding them because "we thought we knew them." Thank God for the leadership of the Holy Spirit!

Second, they do know us! This becomes a barrier in our minds and hearts to keep us from witnessing to them. They know our inconsistencies, our lifestyle, and our apparent lack of spiritual concern for them. We need to break through these barriers and share Christ with them.

When my first wife, Betty, died in West Texas, I was a young pastor with a four-year-old son, Duane. At her funeral a young woman friend of ours was saved. She was married to a man who played the fiddle and operated a dance hall. He would not receive Christ. He said, "What I do is my livelihood. It is the only way I know to make a living." He rejected Christ. I moved away from the area and had no close connection for many years. The man died.

His brother, Ben, had worked with him and played an instrument and sang. I did periodically go back to the area to lead revival meetings. Every time I was in a meeting nearby, Ben came to hear me preach, but I had very little personal contact with him.

It was a cold, snowy winter day and I was back in the area. God spoke to my heart and impressed me to go see Ben. Frankly, I was scared, but I went. He and his nephew were in front of the house working on their travel bus to get it ready for an engagement. We visited and Ben showed me the fiddle that Bob Wills, who was their dear friend, had given them. They had Bob Wills' old travel bus parked nearby. It was like an antique. We had a very interesting visit.

Finally, I asked Ben to get in the car with me where we could stay warm and visit. I got to the point. I said, "Ben, you have come to hear me preach many times and I am grateful. But, I want to ask you to forgive me because I have never personally talked to you about Jesus. Have you come to know him as your personal Savior?"

Ben's answer was that he had received Christ and joined the church when he was a young man. Then, he said something that shook me! He said, "Darrell, I knew you would come. I did not know when, but I knew you would come and talk with me about Jesus!" We had further discussion and a meaningful prayer.

Then I realized why I had gone to see Ben about Jesus. I was thankful for God's conviction in my heart to do it. If I had not, Ben would surely have thought, "Darrell does all this preaching to people, but he does not really care about me." Or, he could have thought, "Darrell goes to all these places preaching, but there is nothing to it, because he is not doing what he preaches about!" Thank God we are not in this alone. He leads us through the guidance of the Holy Spirit.

We are to witness in the marketplace, to our friends, at school, in our neighborhoods, and in our daily traffic pattern.

The great evangelist, D. L. Moody, shared his passion for reaching the lost. He said, "I see every person I meet as though he had a huge 'L' in the middle of his forehead. 'L' for lost and I consider him lost until I know he is saved. I seek to share the Gospel with him."

Dr. Roy Fish once said, "If I am with a person and have conversation, I know I am responsible to direct the conversation toward Jesus and to seek to share Christ with that person."

We find people everywhere we go who need Jesus. We cannot witness to the wrong person. There are just two kinds of people from God's perspective. Man sees many groups: rich and poor; educated and uneducated; different social groups; different races. Man sees many kinds of people. But God sees two groups, the saved and the lost. Everyone is either saved or lost!

If we witness to the saved, we have found a brother or sister in Christ. We can rejoice together. Kathy and I were having dinner in a restaurant. Our server had a name tag, Darrell. I wanted to witness to him, so I began a conversation about his name. I said, "You have a great name! Darrell, is your name; that is my name." He was not impressed! So, I decided to use a little humor. I said, "By the way, are you my other brother Darrell?" I was reaching back to the old television show with my feeble attempt at humor. He was certainly not impressed by that. He was a tall, nice-looking young black man. I am sure he did not want to claim kin to anything that looked like me. Then, I asked, "Do you know Jesus Christ as your Savior and Lord."

"Yes, I do!" he said.

'Then, you are my other brother, Darrell. We are brothers in Christ!" A smile broke across his face and we had a good time visiting. If I had not witnessed to him, I would have missed the joy of knowing this fine brother.

Charles, one of the finest witnesses I have known, was a banker. He told me that everyone who sat across the desk from him wanted to talk about money. But, as he visited with them other problems surfaced. He would deal with them at the point of their real need. He would allow them to express their hearts and if it became appropriate, he would share Christ with them. He led many in his town to Christ through practicing marketplace witnessing. He never violated the confidences of his clients nor manipulated them to open the opportunity to share

Christ. Numerous churches profited greatly by the witness of this faithful Christian witness in the marketplace.

Another effective witness for Christ is a thirteen year old named Jane. Jane's faith was genuine. Many of her schoolmates were disturbed about the problems of teenagers. Jane would listen to them and allow them to open their hearts to her. She would share Jesus with them, lead them to Christ, and invite them to church and Sunday school. Jane was effective in reaching her schoolmates for Christ.

Larry and Rose were our neighbors. We got acquainted and took their children to Sunday school. Rose was Hispanic and a Catholic, but not saved. Hard times hit and they were about to lose their house. We ministered to them and led them to faith in Christ. Rose knew that she could not be baptized because she was Catholic and it would break her mother's heart. They came to church and we prayed with them. Because Christ was in her heart, she knew she needed to obey him by being baptized. She spoke to her mother about it. Surprisingly, her mother was so glad Rose had committed her life to Christ that she encouraged rather than discouraged her. Larry and Rose were baptized and became active witnesses for Christ. Today they are some of our dearest and closest friends. When we witness to neighbors, it works as we are sensitive to the leadership of the Holy Spirit.

We can share Jesus in our marketplace, school, and neighborhood. *God wants every church to implement total penetration of its Jerusalem with the Gospel of Christ.*

Every person and family in the church's Jerusalem (primary ministry area) needs and deserves a witness for Christ and the church. It is a tremendous step forward when a church intentionally decides to discover and reach with the Gospel every home in its community. This will open doors for caring ministry and will attract them to our public proclamation and event attractions. It will utilize the personal presentation of the Gospel through caring witnesses. It will implement the strategy of geographic saturation to find and share Christ with every resident. God will use it abundantly to reach people and grow the church. Church growth is the result of the church being the healthy church-obeying Christ in his mission and commission to reach people who need Christ.

Training and Equipping for Witness

Help God's people to believe that it is God's purpose for them to witness!

There is in every Christian a desire to witness to the lost. They might have gone on so long without witnessing to anyone that the desire has diminished to a spark. But the spark can be fanned by biblical preaching and by involving them in witnessing, and it can become a burning flame. It can be fanned by conducting prayer for evangelism emphasis. Help them get the vision of the church to reach every person in their Jerusalem with the message of Christ for their lives. Communicate this vision and repeat it periodically.

Set as your objective to train and equip every member to share Christ and lead the lost to him.

We want to be successful in our witnessing. Fear of failure keeps many from attempting to witness. From Dr. Bill Bright I learned a definition of successful witnessing that I have used in training Christians. It is confidence as they witness.

Successful witnessing is sharing Christ in the power of the Holy Spirit and leaving the results to God. This definition has three parts: sharing Christ; in the power of the Holy Spirit; leave the results to God. As I teach this definition, I ask, "Which of the three do you like best?" All of the many I have taught to witness say with joy, "Number three!" Leaving the results to God lifts a heavy load from our shoulders. The Holy Spirit is the soulwinner. He is the one who does the converting and gives the new birth. This definition is liberating for witnessing believers. It reduces the fear element.

George Wanted to be Trained to Witness

Many Christians want to witness, but they do not know how. They need to be trained and equipped in how to effectively share Christ with people. One of my dearest friends was George Stout. He has already gone to receive the soulwinner's reward in Heaven. When I met him, I had just become pastor of First Baptist Church in Pasadena, Texas. George came to my office and told me of his passion. He said, "Pastor,

I am sixty-five years old. I could continue to work until I am seventy at the University of Houston as a professor of music. But God has told me 'George, I want you to retire and be available to me to go to anyone to whom I send you to witness them for Christ.' But, I have a problem! I do not know how to do it well. Would you train and equip me? I have asked three pastors to train me, but none ever did."

I was thrilled to the point that my spine tingled! I said, "George, you are talking my language! Be in my office every Monday morning at 8:00 AM. I will show you what I know." George was there every Monday morning. He began to lead people to Christ! Actually, it went both ways. As I trained him, he taught me. He always participated in our witness training schools and seminars like WIN School and People Sharing Jesus Seminar. He learned the witness training materials and began to train others.

But Satan was not pleased. He wanted to stop George from God's mission. Satan tried to divert George from what God had in mind for him. George had been professor of music at the University of Houston with a concentration in piano. He developed and taught the first Piano course ever taught on television. A company in New York City purchased his material for teaching piano lessons on television. They offered him a lucrative contract to direct it for them in New York. Satan was trying to buy George off from God's call. George quickly responded by saying, "Thank you, but no! God has told me, 'George, I want you to be available to me to go to anyone to whom I send you to share Christ with them.' I must do what God has called me to do!"

No doubt God could have used George in New York City. But, God had something more important in mind for him.

George went with me to share in national and international engagements. He led people to Christ and gave testimonies at the events where I preached. Depending on the time allotted to us, he gave his testimony in five minutes, three minutes, or one minute. He never abused the time allotted. He had an eight-word testimony, "Confess and be filled; go tell; do it!" He loved pastors and pastors loved him. He would say, "I am a Pastor's man! I pray for pastors. If you want me to pray for you every day, give me your name and I will." Thousands of pastors gave him their names and he prayed for them.

One cold and rainy Saturday morning, I was dreading Sunday. Baptists and rain don't mix. I anticipated a low day in attendance and outreach. Then George called. He said, "Pastor, I am reporting in. I just went to the hardware store to buy a saw blade. They didn't have one. As I was coming out of the hardware store, I looked down the alley and saw a forlorn-looking woman." What a forlorn-looking woman looks like, I do not know. But, that is what George said. He continued, "I spoke to her. She invited me in and I led her, her husband, and children to Christ. She went next door and got her neighbors. I led them to Christ. She telephoned her sister. Her sister and family came and I led them to Christ. Tomorrow there will be thirteen people on my pew who will come forward and confess Christ as Savior."

Immediately my spirit lifted and God gave me revival in my heart. I could not wait until Sunday! God would give the victory of people confessing Christ. When God's people like George faithfully witness, it will change the life of the pastor! Twenty-three years after I had met George, I preached his funeral on a Christmas Eve. He had led multitudes to Christ and had equipped thousands of Christians to witness.

George's son told me, "Pastor, you did not know my father until he was sixty-five years old. His life began at age sixty-five. He was never the same." Witnessing changes lives! It changes our lives! It changes the lives of people to whom we witness. Like George, all of our people need to be trained and equipped to share Christ.

Many witness-training methods, processes, and programs have been developed that are effective in training people to witness. Some of them are:

People Sharing Jesus Seminar: I developed it and wrote the book, *People Sharing Jesus* and materials to help teach it. They can be seen and ordered through my Web site www.totalchurchlife.net. It takes a nonthreatening, natural, conversational approach in sharing Christ. It has been used by many churches effectively. It is intentional and relational in its approach. It is person-centered, following the model of Jesus, who never approached two people in the same way.

One Verse Evangelism (English and Spanish): It is quick and easy to use. See it at www.sbtexas.com/evangelism.

The Net Complete Kit: See at www.sbtexas.com/evangelism.

Video – Cross and The Crescent: Available at www.sbtexas.com/evangelism.

Video – Mormon Puzzle: Available at www.sbtexas.com/evangelism.

Two-Hour Witness Training: See it at www.sbtexas.com/evangelism.

Evangelism Explosion: EE was written by D. James Kennedy and has been greatly used.

Faith Evangelism: It may be seen at www.lifeway.com/faith.

Share Jesus without Fear: It may be seen at www.lifeway.com.

The Net: It may be seen at www.namb.net in Personal Evangelism.

One-Day Witnessing Workshop: It may be seen at www.namb.net in Personal Evangelism.
Backpack Evangelism: Developed by Lee Rushing. Good for all ages. See it at www.backpackevangelism.com.

Regardless of the program, method, or process that is used, a church should have a witness training event at least every six months. It is good to alternate in using two or three different approaches in witness training. One approach will be effective with some of your people and another with others of your people. They have uniquely different personalities, temperaments, and gifts.

Witness Training Using a Booklet as the Sermon in a Sunday Morning Worship Service

One very simplified approach I used was to train our people using a witnessing booklet like Billy Graham's *Steps to Peace with God*, or *Four Spiritual Laws*, or *Eternal Life*. I have used all of these at different times. How do you do it? Us it at the Sunday morning worship service to train as many people as you can to share Christ.

Order enough booklets for everyone who attends the Sunday morning worship service. Give a copy to every attendee. As you begin the sermon, explain that the sermon will be different and interactive today. Tell them that you will go through this booklet with them. Read the printed material and ask them to read the Bible verses. You will play the role of the witness, and though it may difficult, they will play the role of the lost person. When you come to the prayer to receive Christ, ask them to pray the prayer. Then read through the follow-up pages.

After this explanation I ask, "Why would I do this today? There are two reasons. First, some of you may not yet know Christ as Savior and Lord. I will ask you to receive Christ and confess him today. Second, those of you who are saved know someone who needs Christ. I ask you to pray and share the booklet with that one or someone during the week ahead."

One Sunday when I used *Steps to Peace with God*, a doctor, a specialist in pediatrics, came forward. Several had tried to witness to him. He was polite but had no apparent interest. The doctor said, "Pastor, I prayed the prayer to receive Jesus with you and I am committing my life to him today!"

Often, it is thought that we have to take an intellectual approach to reach someone like the doctor. He is a specialist, an intellectual! But, God used the simplest approach to reach him. Of course, he was a specialist in pediatrics. He could use technical medical terminology and lose me on the second word. But he knew little of the Bible and of theology. A simple presentation from the booklet was understandable and moved his heart. One of my friends who has led many to Christ learned to do it by using such a booklet and still uses it.

People sharing Jesus witness training helps Christians to develop the approach that is comfortable for them and is effective for God to use their unique personalities and gifts. This is a key to training every member to witness. Shelley was one of our members. She is an example of the way God can use us and the uniqueness of our temperament, personality, and gifts to lead people to Christ.

Shelley Led a Hardened Old Man to Christ by Being a Bridge to Him

Shelley is a lovely, blond-haired, and very shy young lady. She wanted to learn to witness in spite of her shyness. As her pastor at Dauphin Way Baptist Church in Mobile, Alabama, my objective was to train and equip every member to lead people to Christ. I led a people sharing Jesus seminar. Shelley participated and went out to visit and share Christ. She led a person to Christ. Joy filled her heart and she began to develop confidence.

An interesting thing happened. She was called on to serve on a jury panel when they were trying an old man, B. J. Hayes, former leader of the Ku Klux Klan in Mobile. A young African-American man had been found hung on a tree just down the street from our church. Hayes was accused as being an accomplice to murder. She saw them mercilessly interrogate the old man. One day he collapsed on the stand. Another time he was stepping down from the witness stand with his cane. A photographer was taking his picture. Mr. Hayes lifted the cane and attacked the photographer who took the picture and it was plastered on front pages of newspapers all over the nation.

Finally, it was ruled a mistrial and B. J. Hayes was freed. Shelley's heart was broken for the old man. She asked our associate pastor to help her find him. They found him on a farm outside of town. Shelley witnessed to him on Saturday. He told her he would meet her in church the next day. Surely enough, on Sunday morning there was Shelley and B. J. Hayes side-by-side on the second row.

God works on both ends at the same time. He had B. J. in church and he gave me a sermon entitled "God's Unfailing Grace." In conclusion I told a story about a notable Texas criminal named Tex Williams. He was being hung at noon for his crimes. When he hit the end of the rope, the rope broke and he hit the dust praising Jesus. He got up and went everywhere preaching, "Paul said he was chief of sinners. Tex Williams is his chief associate. If God could save Paul and Tex Williams, God can surely save you!"

I extended the invitation. The first one down the aisle was B. J. Hayes, tottering on his cane. He said, "Pastor, I have never felt such love! I only wish my wife could have lived to know this love. I want to receive Jesus!" We prayed together and he received Christ. Then, he told me that he had often passed this church building and would say, "Hayes you need to go in there. Then I would say, no, Hayes, you can never go in there. You are not as good as those people! There was a time when I had a million dollars in the bank, but I was not good enough to come in here."

Thank God for a lovely, blond, shy Shelley who became a bridge to reach an old man who had lived his life in hatred for many years. Every Christian can be a bridge for somebody. Many people we meet need such a bridge to come to Christ.

You can be a bridge for someone to come to Christ!

A Format for Training and Equipping Church Members to Witness

- Do adequate preparation. Prepare for the witness training to be the most successful possible. Organize a leadership team to help the pastor prepare the entire church. Begin preparation for the witness training six month ahead of the witness training event.

1. Do extensive prayer preparation.

2. Lead the church to study the Book of Acts with emphases on the Holy Spirit, witnessing, the church, God's promise, the power of the Word of God, and personal relationships.

3. Prepare by pre-enlisting all church leaders and every possible member.

4. Discover as many lost prospects as possible. Conduct a door-to-door witness or survey in the church's Jerusalem. Do an inside the church prospect discovery. Use the "who-do?" cards for members to turn in the prospects they know. The number of people you reach will correspond directly to the number of prospects in the file.

5. Secure the best possible teacher or leader to train the people. The pastor may do it.

6. The pastor must be involved and lead the way. People do what the leader does and what he leads them to do. The speed of the leader is the speed of the team.

7. Plan to do eight to twelve weeks of follow through by meeting and going out to witness on one night per week. A church with many senior adults may need to also have a daytime meeting and witnessing to involve them.

8. Set the dates and time for the training at the best time for the involvement of the most of your people.

• Conduct the witness training seminar or workshop.

1. Schedule it at the best time for your people. Friday through Sunday, Sunday through Wednesday, Saturday and Sunday, or whatever schedule will work to involve the greatest number of your people.

2. Train the people to:
(a) Be assured of their own salvation.
(b) Be filled and controlled by the Holy Spirit.
(c) How to give their own personal testimony.
(d) How to share Christ using a witnessing booklet.
(e) How to share Christ using the Roman road, John 3, or the lifeline presentation.
(f) How to guide a witnessing conversation.
(g) How to make a home visit.
(h) How to guide a person through the conversion experience.

3. Schedule an hour and a half of visitation time. Meet at the church. Set up teams of two or three with no man and woman who are not husband and wife going alone. Assign prospects. Do not let people choose the prospects they will see from the list you have prepared. It will be too time consuming. Place two prospect cards in an envelope and give one to each team person. Give teams envelopes with addresses in the same area to save driving time. The pastor will share for three minutes to encourage the people with God's promise about witnessing. Lead in prayer and send the people out within fifteen minutes.

4. Make the visits and return to the church for report and share time. If you meet at 7:00 PM, people should return by 8:45 PM.

5. The pastor should conduct report and share time. It will extend the teaching time. It is a time of learning from one another. It will be an encouraging time when those who have had a difficult experience will hear of the positive reports from others. We learn from one another. Have a prayer time for the people who have been visited. Dismiss.

7. Some will be late in returning if they have had particularly good visits. The pastor and a leader or two should wait until they return. They will want to tell their story to the pastor and receive his approval and encouragement. This is a critical time for us to train, equip, and encourage your people in witnessing.

• Conduct a weekly follow-through for eight to twelve weeks after the witness training seminar.

1. Use the same prospect assignment procedure as was used in the seminar. Schedule two hours to meet, make the witnessing visits, and report and share time for each week. At the first of the visitation meeting the pastor should review the witnessing material for five minutes, lead in prayer, and send out the teams to visit prospects.

3. Return to the church after one and one-half hours for report and share time. The pastor needs to lead the report and share time. It is a time of encouragement, of continuing to build a climate for evangelism, and of continued learning about witnessing as people share with one another about their experiences. Close with prayer for the people who have been visited.

THIS SIX-MONTH EMPHASIS IN THE LIFE OF THE CHURCH WILL ENGAGE MANY IN THE CHURCH IN CONSISTENTLY WITNESSING IN THEIR DAILY LIVES. IT WILL ASSIST IN BUILDING THE CLIMATE OF EVANGELISM IN THE CHURCH. LOST PEOPLE WILL BE SAVED AND ADDED TO THE CHURCH. THERE WILL BE A STEADY FLOW

OF PEOPLE COMING TO THE PUBLIC PROCLAMATION WORSHIP SERVICES. IT WILL ENHANCE A SPIRIT OF REVIVAL IN THE CHURCH.

REMEMBER THAT THIS IS NOT THE END OF THE PERSONAL EVANGELISM EMPHASIS. IT IS THE BEGINNING. ADDITIONAL TRAINING AND EQUIPPING WILL NEED TO BE DONE PERIODICALLY. THE FIRE THAT HAS BEEN IGNITED WILL TEND TO BURN DOWN AND THERE WILL BE LESS AND LESS PARTICIPATION IF REPETITION OF THE PERSONAL EVANGELISM EMPHASIS AND WITNESS TRAINING IS NOT DONE PERIODICALLY.

PASTORS OFTEN PREACH A GOOD, EVANGELISTIC SERMON AND NO LOST PEOPLE RESPOND TO THE INVITATION TO COME FORWARD AND CONFESS CHRIST. THEY ARE DISAPPOINTED AND WONDER WHY? THE REASON IS NOBODY HAS BEEN LED TO CHRIST DURING THE PREVIOUS WEEK! IF A CHURCH HAS AN ARMY OF WITNESSES LEADING PEOPLE TO CHRIST DURING THE WEEK, SUNDAY WILL BE A HARVEST DAY!

During my years as a pastor, I made evangelistic visits on Saturday. Saturday is one of the best times in the week to find people at home and lead them to Christ. Because of its nearness in time to Sunday, when people are saved on Saturday, they are more likely to come to church on Sunday and confess Christ. I led my staff to meet on Saturday morning for a few minutes of prayer, then each of us would take a member with us for evangelistic visitation.

My major purpose for Saturday evangelistic visitation was that I had made the commitment to God that I would do my best to not stand in the pulpit on Sunday without knowing that someone would come forward to confess Christ. Many times I made visits all day on Saturday!

God honored this commitment. There was seldom a Sunday that no one confessed Christ as Savior and Lord! Our staff joined in this commitment and it changed their lives and the lives of many to whom they witnessed. It also changed the lives of members we invited to be our witnessing partners on those Saturdays.

Equipping and Engaging Members in Witnessing Takes Time

In Rio de Janeiro, Brazil, I trained pastors to use these principles. One pastor lifted his hand and, then, said, "We can't do that! Our people do not get home until 9:00 PM because of the heavy traffic. The work or have home responsibilities on Saturday!"

I asked, "What about Sunday afternoon? You have a great evangelistic service on Sunday night. Why not meet early and spend an hour equipping your people, then go out to witness and practice what they have learned? They could bring people back to the evangelistic service."

"No!" he responded. "We have choir rehearsal on Sunday afternoon."

My question was, "How many members do you have?"

"We have about two hundred fifty members."

"How many choir members do you have?"

"We have about twenty-five in the choir."

My suggestion was, "How about asking your choir to rehearse at another time and for the church body to come together for equipping and evangelizing at this prime time."

The television industry has developed what they call "prime time." Prime time is the time when they have the greatest potential number of viewers. What do they do with their Prime Time? They do priority programming so they can sell more lucrative ads.

Churches also have prime time! It is the time when the greatest numbers of their members are available to be equipped. It is the time when more people in the community are most likely to be at home and can be visited.

We can learn from the television industry. Jesus said in his parable of the unjust steward, "For the sons of this age are more astute than the sons of light in dealing with their own people" (Luke 16:8b HCSB).

Churches can plan to do priority activities at their prime time!

We do have time! Should I say to you in response to an invitation, "No, I can't do that! I don't have time!" You will know that I am lying. I do have time. Both you and I have twenty-four hours per day and seven days per week. I do have time. What I should say is, "No, I can't do that. I have other commitments for that time." I have another priority for this prime time.

Personal presentation of the Gospel by individual members of a church along with geographic saturation, event attraction, and caring ministry will be synergistic in drawing a maximum number of the population of the church's Jerusalem to its public proclamation. It will result in kingdom growth as the people of the church's area are touched and go to other churches in the area. One church's faithfulness to the Commission of Christ will help many churches grow.

CHAPTER EIGHT
Different Ways of Presenting the Gospel

When we talk to people about witnessing, immediately the fear factor comes into play. "I am too shy! I am afraid I will not know what say! I am afraid I will mess up!"

This reminds me of the young man who decided to become a bank robber! He had failed at everything else. He said, "I will do the one thing through which I can make the most money in the fastest way possible. I will be a bank robber!"

He sat up night after night planning the bank robbery, but could never make himself do it. Finally, he said, "I am going to do it today no matter what. I am going to rob the bank." He planned it. He got up early in the morning, but could not force himself to go to the bank. Then, at about noon he drove to the bank parking lot, but he could not force himself out of the car. At 2:00 PM he forced himself out of the car and into the bank. He had a bag for the money and a pistol. He walked to the teller's window. He stuck the money bag in her face, handed her the pistol, and said, "Don't stick with me, this is a mess-up!"

Many believers have a difficult time getting started. The conversation guide is a natural, nonthreatening way to get started and move into a presentation of the Gospel of Christ.

A Conversation Guide to Use in Presenting the Gospel

Getting into a conversation to present the Gospel is difficult for many Christians. My desire is to show how we can use a conversation guide to naturally and in a nonthreatening way converse with a person and move the conversation toward sharing Jesus. The approach is personal, intentional, and relational. Christians are sometimes accused of "button-holing," "collar-grabbing," and a "stuffing-the-Bible-down-their-throat," approach in witnessing. Of course, that is seldom true, but it is the perception of many toward those who witness for Christ.

People need a caring, loving approach that is person-centered rather than forcing a religious conversation on them. We can use a dialogical approach that helps get to know and begin a personal relationship with them. Listening is a key to this approach. You will listen about eighty-five percent of the time and speak about fifteen percent of the time. In doing so, we discover some of their needs and we can share Christ with them at the point of their need. The conversation guide is represented by the acronym as follows: FIRM. F = Family; I = Interests; R = Religion; M = Message.

F for FAMILY: Ask questions and discuss where they grew up and their family. Ask where they live now. Most people enjoy talking about family, their children, their grandchildren, and where they are from.

I for Interests: Ask about and discuss their job, or with young people, about their school. Ask about their leisure, sports, travel, golfing, or fishing. You are getting to know them.

R for Religion: In as natural way as possible ask about their church or religious background. You might ask, "When you were growing up, what church did you attend?" "Have you found a church home since you moved to your neighborhood?" Some may say that they do not have a church and never go. Some may say that they have no church, but they are Muslim, Hindu, or atheist. Their answer makes no difference. You are introducing the subject of religion. You want to bridge the conversation to share about Jesus.

Use a bridge question: You may say, "I am Baptist, but church is not the main thing. A person could be Baptist, Methodist, Muslim, or Mormon. That will not get us to heaven. The main thing is Jesus. May

I ask you a question about Jesus?" If you get their permission to ask the question, they are not offended when you ask.

Bridge question: Have you come to know Jesus Christ in a personal relationship, or are you still in the process? There are three possible answers: yes, no, or I am still in the process! If the answer is yes, you may say, "Wonderful, will you tell me about it?" If they don't want to share their experience, you may ask, "May I share how it happened to me," and share the Gospel with them. If their answer is no, or I am still in the process, ask if you can share with them how they could come to know him?

M for Message: If they give permission, prayerfully decide on the approach you will take and share the Gospel of Christ and ask them to pray and receive him. (A fuller explanation of this approach is in Chapter 4 of *People Sharing Jesus*.)

The conversational approach can be very natural. Whether you are witnessing or not you can use this approach to get acquainted with strangers, new neighbors, or people in the marketplace. In witnessing I have used this approach for many years, and it is as effective today as ever before. Jesus is our model! He conversed with people and then gave God's truth to them. Some followed him. Others turned away. It may well have been that some who turned away followed him later.

How You Can Present the Gospel by Sharing Your Personal Testimony

There is power in sharing your personal testimony. Paul powerfully gave his testimony to the violent crowd that wanted to kill him in Acts 22. King Agrippa was greatly moved by Paul's personal testimony in Acts 26. There are several reasons for its power.

1. You know what happened. You are the specialist on your testimony. It is irrefutable. People cannot say, "No, that did not happen to you." You were there and you know.

2. People will be interested. Two things interest people. First, humor interests people. Second, human interest stories interest people. Secular marketing uses human interest stories extensively. They use them to sell paper towels, toothpaste, automobiles and thousands of other products.

3. Your testimony is unique. There is no other exactly like it. God will use it in unique ways to reach people that possibly no one else could reach.

4. Your testimony will establish empathy with people helping them realize that they too can be saved.

Prepare your salvation testimony under three topics.

1. My life before I came to know Christ.

2. How I received Christ.

3. How Christ makes my life meaningful.

Prepare your personal testimony by writing it briefly under the three topics above so you can share it in one and a half minutes. Why? Because you may not have longer than that in a grocery checkout line, on an elevator, at work, or with a neighbor or friend. Also, people have short attention spans. Making your testimony longer may allow their minds to drift to think about other things while you are speaking. You can always expand it if the occasion permits.

In writing on the first topic, my life before I came to know Christ, share how your life really was. Be careful not to glorify sin if you consider yourself a notable sinner.

In writing on the second topic, how I received Christ, share how you came to Christ. Do it in such a way that the person who shares will know how they can come to Christ and receive him.

In writing on the third topic, how Christ makes my life meaningful, show briefly how you were not perfect, but Christ has been with you since you received him.

Write your testimony and practice sharing it with a family member or friend.

How to Use a Gospel Booklet

There are three reasons for using a booklet.

1. A booklet is simple to use. Anyone who can read can share the Gospel using a booklet. One man who could not read asked a lost person to read it to him. When they came to the page with the prayer, he asked the lost person to pray that prayer and receive Christ. He did pray and receive Christ.

   Jason stopped by for a quick hamburger at a fast food place. Lisa took his order. It was late and business was slow. Jason began to converse with Lisa using the FIRM (Family, Interests, Religion, Message) conversation guide. Lisa expressed an interest in Jesus, saying that she was "In the process of considering coming to Christ." Jason asked her to read through the Gospel booklet with him. Lisa prayed and trusted Jesus. Then she asked Jason to share with her sister who was working in the back. But her sister was busy with her work and could not get free to meet Jason. The next night when Jason returned, he was greeted by a joyful Lisa. Lisa told him that he would not need to talk to her sister. She said, "I took the booklet you left with me and did with my sister what you did with me. She trusted Christ and now both of us are Christians." Jason, Lisa, and her sister shared together with excitement and joy about how to follow Christ as His disciples.

2. A booklet illustrates the Gospel and gives the Scriptures and an explanation of how to receive Christ. The diagrams and illustrations are excellent tools to aid understanding. You can use the highlighted topics and explain the diagrams and lead a person to Christ.

3. Training Christians to use a booklet can be done quickly and easily.

4. Procedure: You may say, "Here is a booklet that has meant much to me. May I share it with you?" Ask the person to hold one side and you hold the other side of the booklet. Use a pen or your finger as a pointer to focus attention on what is being read. You read the print and ask the lost person to read aloud the Scriptures. (Their

reading Scripture keeps them involved. As they read, the Scripture will penetrate their mind in a greater way because they are using three senses, sight, speech, and hearing. If you read them, they use only hearing and may even not be listening.

5. Some advantages of using a booklet in witnessing are: First, the presentation of the Gospel is written in the booklet and does not have to be memorized so that anyone can use it to share Jesus. Second, the approach is simple and thorough in its presentation of the Gospel. Third, the booklet may be left with the person to whom you have witnessed for them to review and gain a better understanding of the decision to receive Christ.

6. There are many different booklets you can use: *Steps to Peace with God*; *Eternal Life*; *Four Spiritual Laws*; *Here's Hope*; and numbers of others.

Presenting the Gospel Using the Roman Road

The book of Romans contains an orderly presentation of the Gospel. It presents the need of sinful humanity, the remedy of sin, and the way to receive Christ and salvation through him. The following passages have been called "the Roman Road to salvation":

- Romans 3:23 HCSB, "For all have sinned and fall short of the glory of God." It shows the universal sinfulness of humanity and the need of every person.
- Romans 6:23 HCSB, "For the wages of sin is death, but the gift of God is eternal life in Christ Jesus our Lord." It shows that the result of sin is death and separation from God eternally. But, God took the initiative to remedy human sinfulness by the gift of his son and through him to provide eternal life.
- Romans 5:8 HCSB, "But God proves His own love for us, in that while we were still sinners, Christ died for us." Because God loves all people in spite of our sins, he provided his own son to die in our place and pay the price for our sins.
- Romans 2:4 HCSB, "Or do you despise the riches of His kindness, restraint and patience, not recognizing that the God's

kindness is intended to lead you to repentance?" God's gracious love draws lost people repent and come to him.

- Romans 10:9-13 HCSB, "If you confess with your mouth, 'Jesus is Lord,' and believe in your heart that God has raised Him from the dead, you will be saved. With the heart one believes, resulting in righteousness, and with the mouth one confesses, resulting in salvation. Now the Scripture says, 'No one who believes on Him will be put to shame,' for there is no distinction between Jew and Greek, since the same Lord of all is rich to all who call upon Him. For everyone who calls on the name of the Lord will be saved."

When a person repents of sin, turns to God, believes in Jesus Christ who died for our sins, was buried, and rose again, and confesses Christ as Lord, he or she will call on the Lord for forgiveness and salvation. According to God's promise he or she is saved.

Dialoguing Through the Roman Road With a Person Who Needs Christ

When you meet a person to whom the Holy Spirit is directing you to witness, use the conversation guide FIRM to converse and guide the conversation toward the message of Christ. Ask the person if you may ask them a question. If they say, "Yes," then ask, "Have you come to know Jesus Christ in a personal relationship or are you in the process?"

If you are visiting in a home, it is good to ask them to allow you to share from their Bible. They will appreciate it and be comfortable using their own Bible and they usually have a story behind how they got the Bible. Let them tell their story. Some may say that they do not have a Bible. You will take your Bible and say, "I would like to give you a Bible." Be sure that you follow up and give them one.

Ask permission to share with them from the Book of Romans. It tells us about our need for Christ and how to be saved. There are some summary verses called the Roman Road that show us how to receive Christ and know for sure we are going to Heaven. Let's share together as we read the passages. (As you do, ask nonthreatening questions.)

WITNESS: Let's turn to Romans 3:23. It is a summary verse for the first three chapters in Romans. Please read the verse aloud. (Reading the verse aloud utilizes the senses of sight, speech, and hearing to impress the Scripture more strongly on the mind of the prospect.)

What does this verse mean to you? (Do not ask what it means. Many lost people do not think they can understand the Bible. So you ask what it *means to him or her.*)

PROSPECT: It means that everyone has sinned.

WITNESS: What about yourself? Would you say that you have sinned against God?

PROSPECT: Yes, I know that I have sinned.

WITNESS: I could not point my finger at you and condemn you as a sinner. I'm a sinner too. Notice that verse 22 says that there is no difference. We have all sinned. We are all in the same boat, and it is a sinking ship. We have all fallen short of what God has for us. The word picture is that of an archer shooting an arrow. It falls short and misses the target. This is what sin is. It is missing the target or the mark that God has set for our lives. Romans 6:23 tells us the result, or wages, of sin is death. If a person works all week, he expects to be paid. According to this verse, what is the payment—wages—of sin?

PROSPECT: It says that the wages of sin is death.

WITNESS: Right. The payment for sin is death. This death is speaking of eternal death or separation from God. Thank God, the verse does not end here! He inserted the word *but.* And what an important word it is. It says that the gift of God is eternal life through Jesus Christ, our Lord. You can't buy, merit, or earn it. The question is "How do you get a gift?"

PROSPECT: You have to accept a gift.

WITNESS: You're right! Jesus is God's gift to us. Through him we have eternal life! Please read Romans 5:8 aloud and see why God gave his son for us.

PROSPECT: (Romans 5:8.) "God gave His Son because He loves us."

WITNESS: Now let's look at Romans 10:9 and 13. It tells us how to come to God and receive his forgiveness and deliverance. These verses indicate three action verbs we are to do. That if you confess with your mouth, "Jesus is Lord," and believe in your heart that God raised him from the dead, you will be saved, for, "Everyone who calls on the name of the Lord will be saved." What are the three things we are to do?"

PROSPECT: Confess that Jesus is Lord, believe God raised him from the dead, and call on him.

WITNESS: May I ask you, do you believe he is God's son and that he died for your sins, that God raised him from the dead, and that Jesus is Lord?

PROSPECT: Yes I do.

WITNESS: Then will you call on him, express your faith to him, and ask him to forgive your sins? It will be a joy for me to pray for you and with you as you pray and receive him. It is not the words of the prayer, but the attitude and faith of your heart that matters to God. This is the kind of prayer that if you can pray and mean it from your heart, God will answer. *Dear Lord, I do believe that you are God's son. I believe you died for me and rose from the dead. I know that I have sinned and fallen short of what you have planned for me. Please forgive me. Come into my heart and help me to be the person you want me to be. Thank you for hearing my prayer and coming into my heart and life. Amen.*

PROSPECT: Yes, I do want to ask him to come into my life.

- If the prospect is not ready to trust Christ and call on him, you may have prayer for him and ask again if he will trust Christ or discuss with him what seems to be standing in the way.
- If the prospect prays and receives Christ, explain what he is to do next. Confess Christ publicly, follow him in baptism, and begin to practice the disciplines of the Christian life including Bible study, daily prayer, regular church attendance, practice tithing and giving, and witness to others for Christ.

Multitudes of people have been led to Christ by witnesses who used the Roman Road presentation to lead them to Christ.

Presenting the Gospel Using John 3:1-18

Using John 3:1-18 to share Jesus is one of the most effective ways to present the Gospel. It is a power-packed passage to deal with those who are lost and their needs.

- It is a direct transcription of Jesus' words leading a man to conversion. His pattern and plan are the best anyone could follow. He is our master, our mentor, and our model in leading people to him.

- It is a single passage that can be read without skipping through several chapters and books that may give the appearance of using proof texts. By simply reading through it, a person can come to understand how to receive life through trusting Christ.

- It is an excellent way to deal with excuses, problems, objections, and concerns before they arise in the conversation with a lost person. This is important. When people position themselves with an argument or excuse, they often feel bound to defend it because of human ego. It is better to deal with it scripturally before they position themselves.

John 3 Addresses Numerous Concerns and Issues

1. Jesus loves and is concerned for the individual (vv.1-3; 16-17).

2. Religion cannot save (vv. 1-3).

3. Church membership cannot save (vv. through the entire passage).

4. Morality, social, economic, or family position cannot save (vv. 1-5).

5. Fear keeps people from Christ (v. 2).

6. Conviction of sin opens people to Christ (v. 2).

7. A person can receive the gift of salvation without having all the answers to spiritual questions (v. 6).

8. Salvation is not by feeling, but by faith (vv. 14-15).

9. Every person, regardless of his or her life situation, must experience the spiritual birth to become a child of God and go to heaven (vv. 3-5).

10. The new birth brings a person into the family of God. This establishes a personal relationship with the father and with everyone in the family of God (vv. 3-5).

11. There is only one way of salvation—through Jesus Christ. There are not many ways. There are not even two ways (v.13).

12. The death of Christ on the cross is necessary for the payment for sin (vv. 14-15).

13. Everyone has been made for eternity. Each will live forever somewhere—in heaven with Christ, or in hell, separated from him (v. 16).

14. God has proven that he is for every person by giving his son (v.17).

15. Spiritually, there are only two groups of people in the world— believers and non-believers. There is no middle ground (v. 18).

God Changed Frank from a Bartender to a Soulwinner

Conversation Guide Through John 3:1-18

The following is an example of a conversational approach for sharing John 3:1-18 (NKJV) with a non-believer. Responses in the dialogue are usually natural and spontaneous. I have used it many times to lead persons to Christ. During a thirty-minute training time, I went through John 3:1-18 in training outreach teams before they made evangelistic visits. When we had completed the training, a young couple went out on visitation. They were elated when they returned to tell us that they dialogued through John 3 with three people. All three gave their hearts to Christ in prayer.

Usually it takes about twenty to thirty minutes to share John 3 with a prospect. It can be done in less time by just reading through the passage and discussing a few of the verses. How much time needed will depend on how much the prospect already knows about the Gospel and what the Holy Spirit is doing in his or her life.

One time I shared John 3 with Frank, an Air Force Sergeant who worked part-time as bartender at the Officer's Club. I asked him if he knew Jesus Christ or was still in the process. He had a can of beer in one hand and a cigarette in the other. He blew smoke toward me and said, "I am no Christian. I love beer and I tend bar where I make more money than on my sergeant's pay. I am not going to give up either beer drinking or bartending."

I said, "Frank, I did not come to talk to you about beer drinking or bartending. I came to talk about Jesus. When you have Jesus in your heart, beer drinking and bartending will fall into the right place in your life. May I share with you a passage about Jesus in John 3?" He agreed. The following is the conversation guide, which you can use by simply dialoguing through the passage with a prospect as I did with Frank.

DARRELL: Frank, this is the greatest sermon ever preached. Of course it was preached by Jesus. We usually think of great sermons being preached by an outstanding evangelist like Billy Graham to a multitude of people in a stadium or large arena. But this sermon was given by Jesus to just one man in the middle of the night. This says that he loves every individual, including you, that he would have come just for you! Now, please read aloud verse one.

FRANK: There was a man of the Pharisees named Nicodemus, a ruler of the Jews.

DARRELL: If you had lived next door to Nicodemus, you would have thought that he had it all. He appeared to be ideal. Yet all of his fine qualities did not change the fact that he had a deep need. He was religious, a Pharisee. He was rich. He was respectable, a ruler of the Jews. But none of these qualities filled the need of his heart. He saw in Jesus what he needed but did not have.

Verse two says that Nicodemus came to Jesus in the night. Why do you think he came at night?

FRANK: I think he was afraid someone might see him.

DARRELL: I think you are right! He was afraid of what others might say or do. Fear and peer pressure sometimes keep people from coming to Christ. It kept me from coming to him for quite some time. (This would be a good time to share your own experience.) Has that ever happened to you? Have you ever felt like that?

FRANK: Yes, I have. When I was young, I wanted to receive Jesus, but my friends and some of my family would have laughed at me and I never did. (Give the prospect an opportunity to express his fear and deal with it.)

DARRELL: There may have been another reason he came at night. (The purpose of this thought is to lead the prospect to realize his or her own sin.) Nicodemus might have come at night because of conviction for his sin. In the stillness of the night, with no distractions, he had to face the loneliness of his spiritual emptiness. When he came face-to-face with himself, he got up and came to Jesus.

Nicodemus did not want to expose the superficiality of his spiritual life, so he attempted to flatter Jesus by saying, "Rabbi, we know that you are a teacher come from God; for no one can do these signs that you do unless God is with him." Jesus brushed aside his compliment and got right to the point. He saw right into the heart of Nicodemus. John 2:25 HCSB says, "He did not need that anyone to testify about man; for He Himself knew what was in man." He sees into my heart and yours. He knows our thoughts and everything we do.

(At this point ask the prospect to read verse three aloud.) Here is a verse where Jesus tells Nicodemus what is really important.

FRANK: Jesus answered and said to him, "Most assuredly, I say to you, unless one is born again, he cannot see the Kingdom of God."

DARRELL: What does this verse mean to you? (Do not ask him to interpret or give its meaning. Ask what it means to him or her.)

FRANK: It just means to me that to go to heaven you have to be born again.

DARRELL: The first time I heard about being "born again" I did not know what it meant. Like Nicodemus in verse four, I thought it meant that you had to go back into your mother's womb and be born all over again and get a new start. Nicodemus' problem was that he trusted his birth as a descendent of Abraham to good parents and his standing as a religious leader to make him right with God.

Jesus tells him in verse five that one must be born of "water and of the Spirit" to enter heaven because "that which is born of flesh is flesh and of the Spirit is Spirit." The water birth is the flesh birth through one is born physically and becomes a member of the human family. But to be born of the Spirit one is born into the family of God and is a child of God. When a baby is born, it is encased in a bag of water. When birth happens, the water breaks and the baby is born. The Spirit birth happens when the Holy Spirit comes into the person's heart and does the miracle of bringing the person into the family of God. (When we hear the word "water" in connection with religion, we usually think about Baptism. You may choose to use this opportunity to explain Baptism, but say that this verse does not speak of Baptism.)

Through the new birth a person becomes a child of God and is a part of the family of God. This establishes a personal relationship with the Father and all of the children of God. The spiritual birth is the miraculous foundation for healthy relationships in all of life.

At this point Nicodemus' eyes must have popped out on stems. In verse seven, Jesus said, "Do not marvel that I said to you, you must be born again." Then, in verse eight, he used an illustration of the wind. (Ask the prospect to read verse eight and ask, "How do we know the wind is blowing? We cannot see it. We don't know where it comes from or where it is going.")

FRANK: We know the wind is blowing because we feel it and see the evidence of it.

DARRELL: This is like being born of the Spirit. You can't see the Holy Spirit. You can't understand all the Spirit does. But you can feel his presence as he convicts you and draws you to Jesus. You experience the changing work he does in your heart.

(Read verse nine.) In verse nine, Nicodemus asked the question you or I would have asked, "How can these things be? How can this happen to me?" In verse ten, Jesus gently rebuked him, "Are you a teacher in Israel, and do not know these things?" Then in verse thirteen, Jesus answered the question about how it can happen for you and me. This verse indicates that the only one who can go to heaven is the one who came from heaven. Who would you say this is talking about? Who came from heaven?

FRANK: I guess it is talking about Jesus. He came from heaven!

DARRELL: Yes! The question is, "If Jesus is the only one who is qualified to go to heaven, then how is it possible for you and me to get to heaven?

FRANK: Well, the only way would be through Jesus.

DARRELL: Yes, that's correct, we have to be in Christ! My illustration is that I received an invitation to preach and teach in Brazil. The time came to leave. My wife, Kathy, drove me to the Gulf of Mexico. I got out and began to swim to Brazil. Do you believe that? No! I would never have made it swimming. I found that an airplane was scheduled to go to Sao Paulo, Brazil. I bought a ticket. At the airport I looked out of the window and saw them working on the plane! A man in a uniform and little cap passed me. They said he was the pilot. He did not look any smarter than me. Would I get on the plane? Crisis time! I decided and got on the plane. The plane got off the ground and I stood up and began to flap my arms to help it along. No, I did not. I buckled my seat belt and leaned back and rested. We arrived in Sao Paulo. All I did was get in something that was going there! To go to heaven we must be "in the one who is going there."

"If anyone is in Christ, there he is a new creation" (2 Corinthians 5:17 HCSB). The only one who will go to heaven is the one who came from heaven—Jesus! We must be in him by faith.

FRANK: Then, the only way I can go to heaven is to know Christ and be in him.

DARRELL: You are right! In verses fourteen through sixteen Jesus tells us how it happens. He draws an illustration from the history of Israel. The people of Israel were in the wilderness. God miraculously provided food and water for them, but they continued to murmur and complain against the Lord. So God disciplined them by sending a plague of snakes into their camp. When the snakes began to bite the people and they were dying. Moses interceded in prayer. God told him to mold a snake out of brass and raise it on a pole in the middle of the camp. When the people were bitten, they were to look to the brass snake on the pole and God would heal them. There was no magic in the brass snake. God healed as they responded by faith to look.

Jesus applied this incident to his being lifted up on the cross. Whoever has been bitten by the serpent bite of sin and death is flowing in their veins, if they will look by faith to him who was lifted up on the cross and died for their sins, Christ will forgive their sins and give them eternal life. Then he gave that wonderful verse, John 3:16 HCSB, "For God loved the world in this way; He gave His One and Only Son, so that everyone who believes in Him will not perish but have eternal life." Now, Frank, please read verse seventeen and tell me what you think."

FRANK: "For God did not send His Son into the world to condemn the world, but that the world through Him might be saved."

I think that Jesus does not condemn me, but wants to save me.

DARRELL: That is certainly true! Now, we will read verse eighteen and he tells how to be saved. As we read it, note that God sees only two groups of people. Who are they and what does it say about them?

"He who believes in Him is not condemned; but he who does not believe is condemned already, because he has not believed in the name of the only begotten Son of God." Who are the two groups?"

FRANK: Those who believe and those who do not believe.

DARRELL: What does it say about the believer?

FRANK: The believer is not condemned!

DARRELL: What about the non-believer?

FRANK: The non-believer is condemned already because he has not believed.

DARRELL: Now, may I ask you a personal question about that? I don't want to embarrass you. But in which of the two groups would you say you are right now? (The answer may be, "A believer. Or a non-believer. Or, I do believe, but…. Whatever the answer may be, you can deal with the answer that has been given.)

FRANK: I am a non-believer!

DARRELL: Frank, I want to ask you now to become a believer!

Now for the rest of the story! Frank did not receive Christ that day. I had prayer for him and his family and left. The next Sunday night Frank and his family were in church. At the invitation he and his wife, Nancy, came forward. They said, "We believe in Jesus Christ and want to accept him as our Savior and Lord!" I did not ask Frank if he would quit bartending and beer drinking. I prayed with both of them and they received Christ.

The next day Frank submitted his resignation to the Officer's Club and told them why! He witnessed to the owner and workers at the bar. He began to lead Airmen to Christ week by week. Frank used John 3 to share with everyone he could. Revival broke out on the Air Base and many came to Christ.

You may not do the dialogue the way I did it with Frank and have done it with many others. You can read through with a minimum amount of dialogue and come to verse eighteen. It is the invitation verse. Use it to "draw the net" and ask them to pray and receive Christ. You may add John 1:12 to ask them to receive Christ.

Using the Lifeline Presentation

The lifeline presentation uses a visual as well as audible presentation of the Gospel. It is a powerful presentation because when you use it, you share the plan of salvation simply and understandably. When I developed it, I used it with children. It was effective, so I decided to use it with adults and young people. It was equally effective with them. In presenting it you can do it briefly and simply. However, it has the potential for you to use it with theological depth and in seminary level theological terminology. I used it as the basis for writing an entire book, *The Doctrine of Salvation*, published by Convention Press, Nashville, TN.

In a small church I taught about two hundred people how to share Christ using the lifeline. Children sat at the front. I led them to practice sharing with one another and next we went on the streets to witness. When we returned to report and share, they reported forty-two people had prayed to receive Christ. I asked individuals to lift their hands and hold up as many fingers as the number of people who received Christ through their witness. A twelve year-old girl, Regina, was very excited as she lifted her hand and held up three fingers. She told about going to three homes and sharing the lifeline presentation with a person in each. All three prayed and received Christ. If twelve-year-old Regina after being trained for thirty to forty minutes, could use it to share Christ and lead three people to Christ, surely every church member can do it.

How to Use the Lifeline Presentation as a Gospel Illustration

The illustration may be presented using a pen, pencil, and a piece of paper, napkin, or lightweight card. If these are not available, you may use your hand and finger.

Ask, "May I share with you about how to come to know Christ as your Savior and Lord? I will illustrate it using my pen and this piece of paper.

"Romans 3:9 says that, 'All humanity is under sin.' As an illustration, the paper will represent sin. If I place my pen *under* the paper, it represents humanity being 'under' sin"

"On the other hand, where is God? I place my pen above the paper. God is holy and righteous. He is above sin.

Holy God

Sin Barrier

Sinful Humanity

Holy God

Sin Barrier

Sinful Humanity

"One who has sinned may attempt to reach God." (Using your pen to represent sinful people, move it up toward God. It will collide with the paper representing the impenetrable sin barrier that separates us as sinful humanity from God.)

"There is no difference, we have all sinned. To be under sin is a horrible place to be. Under sin we are: separated from God (Romans 6:23); without God, without Christ, without hope (Ephesians 2:12); spiritually blind (2 Corinthians 4:3-4); condemned already (John 3:18); enemies of God (Romans 5:10); children of the devil (John 8:44); no peace (Romans 3:17 and Isaiah 57:20-21); the wrath of God abides on them (John 3:36).

"Sinful people attempt to reach God in many ways. These may include good works, reformation, morality religious performances, and philanthropy. But it is impossible for one who has sinned to reach holy God in these ways. All the religions of the world are man attempting to reach God through their own means—self effort! Christianity is unique! Man cannot break through the sin barrier. Christianity reveals that because of His love, God took the initiative to come to us in and through the person of Jesus Christ, his son.

"If we physically die under sin, we are spiritually dead already and will be in hell forever. Hell is the place where the 'fire is never quenched and the worm never dies.' It is the place of eternal suffering, sorrow, and separation from God. There is unbearable, yet, inescapable suffering.

"The only possibility for sinful people to come through the sin barrier and receive life from God is for God in his love to intervene in the human situation. Under sin, we are spiritually dead. God is the only source of life. Jesus Christ is the 'way, the truth, and the life' (John 14:6). He is the only lifeline to God!

"God did what human beings could never do! In the person of Jesus Christ, his son, God came into the human situation. He penetrated the sin barrier to identify himself with humanity and to live a sinless life on earth. He went to the cross and died as He paid the price for our sins. There he 'bore our sins in His own body' (1 Peter 2:24 NKJV), providing the way for sinful people to come to God through him. "

(Penetrate the paper with your pen to represent Jesus coming into the human situation. It will form a cross representing Jesus dying for our sins to be "the way, the truth, and the life." Sinful people can now come to God through him.)

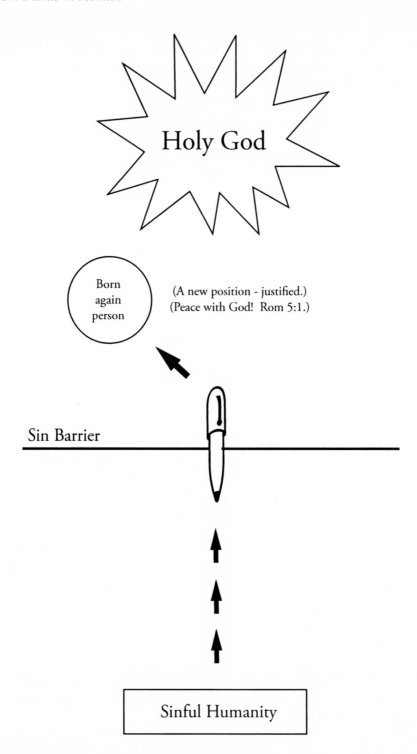

Holy God

Born again person

(A new position - justified.)
(Peace with God! Rom 5:1.)

Sin Barrier

Sinful Humanity

Sinful people, through repentance and faith, come to Christ by praying and receiving him. They are forgiven, and become children of God (Acts 20:21). You can receive the gift of salvation by repenting (turning from your sin and self-efforts) and by faith coming to Christ. You must trust him as your Savior and Lord. You will be born again as a child of God. You will have a new position of being justified and made right with God. You will have peace with God and begin your new life on your way to heaven.

Eight Men Receive Christ Through Lifeline Presentation in a Bar in Brazil

The lifeline presentation works in every kind of context. Other Christians and I have used it in homes where we were called to come, in homes where we dropped by, at the door when we went door-to-door, in offices and businesses, in schools, on airplanes, and in restaurants. It has been done with groups. At Fleming Island, Florida I shared it with five men who received Christ. I stood in a doorway of a bar in Pinheiro, Brazil and presented the lifeline to eight men who stood at the bar. All eight prayed and received Christ.

I shared the lifeline at the funeral of an IBM Executive. Six people lifted their hands that they had prayed with me and received Christ. A short time ago a young man and his bride-to-be asked me to share the Gospel and give an invitation at their wedding. I did so using the lifeline. Two people lifted their hands that they were receiving Christ.

Jae Receives Christ Through Lifeline

On my way to train pastors, churches, and leaders in People Sharing Jesus Seminars, Witness Saturation, and Total Church Life Strategy Seminars, I found myself in a middle seat on the airplane. I detest middle seats. I have a million and five hundred thousand miles with that airline. There is a request in my profile to always have an aisle seat. I was grumbling to myself. What if a huge, three hundred pound guy sits by me and laps over into my seat all the way to Brazil.?

In a little while a tall, slender, red-haired young lady sat down beside me. That made the middle seat not so bad. I got acquainted with Jae. I used the FIRM conversation guide to get acquainted. Starting with F for Family, I asked her where she was from. She said, "Australia."

I asked, " How did you decide to come to Houston?"

She said, "I married a man from Houston and we live here."

Now on to "I" for Interests. I asked, "Where are you headed?"

"To Madrid, Spain," she responded. "You see, I play professional women's basketball for the Arizona women's team and am going to play with the Madrid team for a month."

"Wow," I said, "I am in the presence of a celebrity." We discussed women's basketball.

How will I get into the "R" for Religion subject? But she did it for me.

She asked, "Where are you going?"

"To Brazil" I answered.

Jae asked, "Do you work for a company there?" I answered, "No, not exactly. I am going to train pastors, churches, and leaders to share Jesus and lead people to know Christ as Savior and Lord."

"That is interesting. How long have you been doing this? And how did you get started?" she asked. (She asked the right questions!)

I told her that I had been doing that kind of thing for a long time. I started when I was young and planning to go to Texas A&M to get a degree in veterinary medicine and make enough money to buy a cattle ranch, but God changed my life and direction. He called me to preach and lead people to Christ. I learned that every Christian is a missionary to lead people to Christ out where we live, work, and play. I went to Baylor University. I have been doing it ever since.

"Jae, may I ask you a personal question?"

"Yes," she responded.

"Jae, have you come to know Jesus Christ in a personal way or are you still in the process?"

"I am in the process! You see my husband is a Baptist. His mother has been after me." Jae said.

I asked, "May I show you how you can come to have a personal relationship with Jesus and really know him?"

"Yes, I want you to show me." (By that time I had a coke and a napkin. I took the napkin and my pen and showed her the lifeline presentation. Her eyes never left the pen and napkin. God moved in her heart.)

I said, "Jae, if you would pray and ask God to forgive you of your sins and for Christ to come into your heart, he will do it. If I could, I would do it for you, but I could not."

Jae said, "No, I would have to do it myself."

Then, I said, "Jae, I could pray with you as you call on him yourself. Could we do it?"   She answered, "Yes, I want to." (I prayed briefly. Then Jae prayed and asked God to forgive her and told him she was receiving Jesus.)

She looked up and said, "I am receiving Jesus." Tears were streaming down her cheeks and a smile was on her face at the same time.

Then, Jae said a beautiful thing, "Darrell, I am going to be a missionary to women's basketball!"

What a joy to see what God does when the Gospel is presented in the power of the Holy Spirit!

Beautiful Baptism

Explaining Baptism to Present the Gospel

"One picture is worth a thousand words" is true with reference to baptism. Baptism as taught and commanded by Jesus in the New Testament is a clear witness to his saving power. It not only confirms the commitment of a believer, but it also captivates the attention and interest of lost people.

It was my first Sunday as Ray's pastor. He accepted Christ and was baptized the next Sunday. The third Sunday his twelve-year-old friend came to me saying, "I saw Ray baptized, and I need Jesus, too." It was a special joy to explain baptism to him and lead him to experience faith in our crucified and risen Lord.

Calvin was a businessperson in our town. In casual conversation one day he remarked, "You Baptists dunk people in your church, don't you?" His remark was quite natural since his religious background was one of "infant baptism" by sprinkling.

My response was as casual as his question, "Yes, Calvin we do dunk people. May I share with you about why we do it this way? May I share with you about Bible baptism? It explains the way we baptize."

It is good for us not to attack nor even discuss churches of other denominations about their mode of baptism. To do so can easily alienate the person with whom you are sharing. Focus on what the Bible says about baptism. I prefer to call it "Bible baptism."

I continued my conversation with Calvin. We shared in reading Bible verses (Romans 6:3-5, Mark 1:9-10, and Matthew 3:16-17) about baptism. I explained the meaning of immersion and asked, "Has this experience happened in your life?"

The result was joyful as Calvin received Christ and followed him in Bible baptism, believer's baptism. Many lost people like the twelve-year-old boy and like Calvin can be led to Christ through presenting the Gospel by explaining baptism.

Why Explain Baptism to a Lost Person

The value of presenting the Gospel through an explanation of baptism is manifold. There are several reasons this is true:

- Many, both within and outside the church, are interested in baptism. People from ritualistic religious backgrounds have a particular interest. Bible baptism by immersion is the church's most beautiful and impressive ritual in speaking to the lost as well as to true believers in denominations that do not practice Bible baptism.

- Lost people are often open to an explanation of baptism. The same people may feel threatened and become defensive when other approaches of Gospel presentation are attempted. Using an object lesson to depict baptism breaks down barriers.

- Baptism teaches the Gospel. The Bible is filled with memorials of significant events and acts of God in the lives of his people. Israel had crossed the Jordan River on dry ground as God miraculously held back the waters creating flood conditions upstream. Joshua instructed them to build a memorial of twelve stones brought from the middle of the Jordan where the priests had stood with the Ark of the Covenant.

  Joshua instructed, "In the future when your descendants ask their fathers, 'What do these stones mean?' tell them, 'Israel crossed the Jordan of dry ground.' For the Lord your God dried up the Jordan before you until you had crossed over. The Lord your God did to the Jordan just what He had done to the Red Sea when he dried it up before us until we had crossed over. He did this so that all the peoples of the earth might know that the hand of the Lord is powerful and so that you might always fear the Lord your God" (Joshua 4:21-24 NIV).

Baptism is the beautiful memorial left by Jesus to depict his death, burial, and resurrection. It reminds the believer of his or her experience of salvation every time a new believer is baptized. It sows the seed of the Gospel as lost people view it and have it explained. It serves as a means to lead lost people to a saving knowledge of Christ.

Those who do not receive Christ immediately will have had the Gospel shared with them. The Word of God will have been received in their hearts. The Holy Spirit will continue to nurture the Word in their hearts. We can trust God to use the explanation of baptism for His glory.

• Baptism convicts of sin. Using baptism to explain the death of Christ on the cross for sinful humanity is a piercing sword of the Holy Spirit to bring conviction. The explanation of the old, dead sin life being buried with Christ as a new believer experiences his forgiveness and new life brings further conviction.

• Baptism confirms a person's commitment to Christ. While baptism does not have saving value, it does give assurance of salvation to the obedient believer. Many believers testify that their full assurance of salvation came as they were baptized.

A Dialogical Presentation of the Gospel Using Baptism

Introductory Conversation: Begin the conversation by dialoguing through FIRM.

WITNESS: May I share with you about Bible baptism? (Prospects may respond that they have been baptized. If so, ask the prospect to share with you about the experience. Often, they will say they do not remember since it happened when they were infants. Do not discuss their "baptism." Focus on what it meant to them. You may say, "Then, your baptism might have been meaningful to your parents, but remember nothing about it? May I share with you the meaning of Bible baptism?")

PROSPECT: Yes, I have never understood baptism.

WITNESS: Let us look together at what the Bible teaches.

Bible Baptism is the Believer's Baptism

Only the person who has believed in Christ and has been born again is qualified to be baptized. If the person immersed is not saved, the immersion is not true baptism. All it means is that you got "dunked and wet!" In every recorded case in the Bible, salvation preceded baptism. In the instructions given by the Bible, believing on Christ is given as a prerequisite for baptism.

The following Scriptures teach believer's baptism:

- On the day of Pentecost, Peter called the people to repentance and commitment to Christ. As a climax to the message, Acts 2:38 and 41 HCSB says, "Repent," Peter said to them, "and be baptized, each of you, in the name of Jesus the Messiah for the forgiveness of your sins, and you will receive the gift of the Holy Spirit ... So those who accepted his message were baptized, and that day about three thousand were added to them."

- Phillip was directed by the Spirit from Samaria into the desert, where he led a man who was traveling in a caravan from Jerusalem to Ethiopia to Christ. Acts 8:36-38 HCSB shares the rest of the story, "As they were traveling down the road, they came to some water. The eunuch said, 'Look, there's water. What would keep me from being baptized?' And Phillip said, 'If you believe with all your heart, you may.' And he replied, 'I believe that Jesus Christ is the Son of God.' Then, he ordered the chariot to stop, and both Philip and the eunuch went down into the water and he baptized him."

- Before he ascended back to the Father, Jesus sent his followers into the world on a mission. His words of commission are, "Go, therefore, and make disciples of all nations, baptizing them in the name of the Father and of the Son and of the

Holy Spirit, teaching them to observe everything I have commanded you" (Matthew 28:19-20 ʜᴄsʙ).

In each of these key passages those who were baptized *first* believed on the Lord Jesus Christ and committed their lives to him.

Bible Baptism Requires the Immersion of a Believer

The biblical mode of baptism is immersion. Three biblical truths indicate the requirement of immersion as the proper method of baptism.

- The Greek word for baptize is "baptizo." Its meaning is "to dip in or under." In every case in the New Testament where baptism takes place, this word is used. The question arises as to why the word was not translated "to dip or to immerse." The answer is the King James translators chose to transliterate rather than translate it. They brought the Greek letters over into their English equivalents and left the interpretation of the meaning to the reader. To baptize, then, is to immerse a believer under the water.

- The setting of biblical baptism demands immersion. In each case of a New Testament baptism, it was by immersion.

- *Jesus was baptized by immersion.* "After Jesus was baptized, He went up immediately from of the water" (Matthew 3:16 ʜᴄsʙ).

"In those days Jesus came from Nazareth in Galilee and was baptized *in the Jordan by John.* As soon as He *came up out of the water,* He saw the heavens being torn open and the Spirit descending on him like a dove. And a voice came from heaven: 'You are My Beloved Son; I take delight in You!'"(Mark 1:9-10 ʜᴄsʙ)

Phillip immersed the Ethiopian eunuch after he was saved.

"Both Phillip and the eunuch *went down into the water* and he baptized him. When *they came up out of the water,* the Spirit of the Lord carried Phillip away, and the eunuch did not see him any longer. But he went on his way rejoicing" (Acts 8:38-39 HCSB).

"John also was baptizing in Aenon near Salim, because there was plenty of water there" (John 3:23 HCSB). Plenty of water was needed to immerse the person being baptized.

- The symbolism of baptism required immersion. Biblical baptism symbolizes a death, a burial, and a resurrection. "Therefore buried with him by baptism into death in order that, just as Christ was raised from the dead by the glory of the Father, so that we too may walk in a new way of life" (Romans 6:4 HCSB).

Bible Baptism is a Symbol

Baptism is a beautiful expression of faith. It is symbolic of two things. It symbolizes an *event*—the event of the death, burial, and resurrection of Jesus. It symbolizes an experience—the experience of the believer's death to an old life of sin, the burial of the old life, and the rising again with Christ to a new life (Romans 6:3-5).

Let me illustrate using two pens:

WITNESS: When you are baptized, you will stand with the pastor in the water. (Hold the pens or use your index fingers upright and side-by-side. Do not say, "If you are baptized." Be positive! Say, "When you are baptized.")

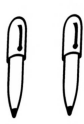

WITNESS: The pastor will gently lower you under the water and raise you up. If it has really happened in your life, you are saying symbolically that you believe Christ died for your sin, was buried, and rose again. You are saying that regardless of what others may do, you have committed your life to live for him. If you are not already saved, the immersion in the water is meaningless. It does not save you. (As you share about the death and burial of Christ, lower one of the pencils until it is horizontal. As you share about the resurrection, raise the pencil up again. You may ask, "Isn't this a beautiful picture?")

Baptism symbolizes an event: the death, burial, and resurrection of Jesus.

When you are standing straight up in the water, the water crosses your body forming a cross. It symbolizes Jesus dying on the cross. At this point cross one of the pens with the other and ask, "What does this form?" Answer, "A cross."

Events Of Jesus' Death, Burial, and Resurrection
Pictures Jesus on the cross.

Lowered under the water, symbolizes the death and burial of Jesus.

Raising the pen symbolizes the resurrection of Jesus.

Baptism symbolizes an *experience*. It symbolizes the death of the believer to an old life of sin, the putting away of the old life, and the resurrection to a new life in Jesus Christ. Use the demonstration with your two pens again.

Without Jesus a person is dead in trespasses and sins.

Believer identified with Christ in His death burial.

Standing in the water. Pen is held. Use other pen to cross the first straight up as water crosses the body.

Pictures the old dead life.

Drawing: Lower Pen under the water.

Drawing: Pictures the Burial of the old dead life.

Resurrection to a new life in Christ.

Resurrection

Raise the Pen to show resurrection.

Pictures new cleansed life raised up with Christ.

WITNESS: Bible baptism is the beautiful expression of what Jesus did for us and what he has done in us. How do you feel about this?

PROSPECT: It is truly beautiful!

WITNESS: Have you had this experience in your own life? Would you like for it to happen? It would be a joy to me to pray with you and for you as you pray and receive him into your life.

After prayer, you may further explain the commitment expressed in the following way:

Baptism today means less to many people than it did to early Christians. Today, in most cases baptism is socially acceptable. For early Christians, it was dangerous. Jesus had just been crucified. Their baptism declared, "I believe that the crucified one is Lord. He died for me and rose again. I have committed my life to follow him no matter what may happen."

For early Christians it meant social ostracism. They were often rejected by their family, friends, and community. It sometimes meant economic boycott, and they were fired from jobs. It meant physical danger. Many were persecuted. Some were put to death.

Through baptism the Christian is saying, "Jesus is my Lord. I will follow him no matter what anyone else may do, even if it means my death. Nothing can change the fact that Jesus is my Lord! I belong to him."

Baptism beautifully presents the Gospel of Christ and offers an opportunity to lead people to Christ!

Sharing about baptism can be used to lead a non-believer to Christ or it can be used with other presentations like giving your testimony, or sharing the Roman road or John 3. If baptism has not been explained before a new believer receives Christ, it is most important to do so soon after he or she has received Christ. Understanding baptism will help the new believer grow in Christ. He or she will obey Christ in baptism.

CHAPTER NINE
Synergistic Evangelism in Local Churches

As a local church utilizes the five biblical techniques seen in the Book of Acts to reach the lost for Christ, it will balance its evangelistic outreach. Using the five techniques—public proclamation, caring ministry, event attraction, geographic saturation, and personal presentation—will involve a maximum number of members. It will enable the church through the Word of God and the work of the Holy Spirit to impact its community, and to create a God-consciousness in homes and families, and to result in people being open to the Gospel of Christ throughout the church's primary ministry area (its Jerusalem). Through the power of this synergistic approach as is proven in the Book of Acts, multitudes will be reached for Christ.

Public proclamation is a part of every church's regular schedule. Some churches use public proclamation in such a way as to say, "for members only." The focus is on the members of the church. In such cases few if any lost people will be reached for Christ. Other churches do have evangelistic preaching and extend an evangelistic invitation in the worship services. But, still few lost people are reached. Why? Lost people are not there!

For public proclamation to be effective in reaching the lost for Christ, lost people must be present for the preaching of the Gospel.

Without the other four evangelistic techniques, very few lost people will attend the church's worship services. Public proclamation alone will be minimally effective in reaching people for Christ if the synergism of the other four evangelistic techniques is not utilized.

Caring ministry that involves members reaching out to hurting people in the community will enhance the number of lost people who attend the church's worship services. This will increase the number of lost people who receive Christ as Savior and Lord.

However, all churches do some caring ministry. But, often churches are introverted and do their caring ministry within the membership of the church rather than reaching out into the community to care for the non-churched in the community. Making the caring ministry evangelistic is the key to reaching the lost for Christ to whom members are ministering. If members involved in caring ministry are led to be intentional in leading people to whom they are ministering for Christ, it will be evangelistic. If they are trained to lead them to Christ, many can be reached. Most of those led to Christ will come to the public proclamation worship service and confess their faith. This will synergistically multiply the evangelistic effectiveness of the church. More lost will be reached through the combined witness of public proclamation and caring ministry.

Event attraction can attract the community. Events that are a mighty work of God will enhance the evangelistic outreach of the church. The event should be publicized throughout the area. Members should invite their families, friends, and acquaintances. The church should contact every prospect through visitation, by mail, by e-mail, and in any way possible. If the church will register every attendee and follow up with them, many can be reached for Christ. Often, if they are followed up on, many will attend the public proclamation worship services at the church and can be reached for Christ. The events can produce a wealth of prospects for the prospect file who can be ministered to and witnessed to periodically until they come to Christ. Public proclamation is synergistically enhanced by event attraction. What would be the percentage of effectiveness in evangelistic outreach by these three, public proclamation, caring ministry, and event attraction? My estimate would be a very low percentage—perhaps twenty-five percent of maximum effectiveness. That is merely a guess, but I think it is close based on years of observation. However, if you add the other two, the increase in effectiveness will greatly multiply.

Geographic saturation can add another thirty-five percent to the effectiveness of the church in reaching the lost for Christ and seeing them come into the church. As the church saturates its community with the Gospel and information about the church, it creates a spiritual concern in the people of the community and an interest in the church. As the church does door-to-door witness and survey and goes to every home and every apartment to get acquainted with the people and share the Gospel, it will discover multitudes of prospects and opportunities for caring ministry. Their information will be included in the church prospect file. They can be followed up periodically. It will greatly increase the number of new prospects who come to the public proclamation worship services. No one will know why they came, but they came because someone from the church contacted and invited them. Sometimes their visit to the church may be a year, two years, or even longer after the original contact. God has dealt with them! They began to think "God, I need God." As they thought "God," they thought of your church because someone from your church recently touched their lives for Christ and your church. Geographic saturation causes the church not only to add to the church those who are being saved, but to experience multiplication evangelism as multitudes are reached.

The addition of people to the church changed to multiplication in the early chapters of Acts. "So those who accepted his message were baptized, and that day about three thousand people were <u>ADDED</u> to them" (Acts 2:41 HCSB).

"And every day the Lord <u>ADDED</u> to them those who were being saved" (Acts 2:47b HCSB). After geographic saturation had been effected in Jerusalem, the word "added" changed to "multiplied."

"Didn't we strictly order you not to teach in this name? And look, you have filled Jerusalem with your teaching, and are determined to bring this Man's blood on us!" (Acts 5:28 HCSB) They had saturated Jerusalem with the Gospel. Here the enemies of Christ admit and accuse the disciples for spreading the Gospel.

"So the preaching about God flourished, the number of the disciples in Jerusalem <u>MULTIPLIED</u> greatly in Jerusalem, and a large group of the priests became obedient to the faith" (Acts 6:7 HCSB). Geographic saturation works! The synergism of the evangelistic techniques through the work of the Holy Spirit caused multitudes to be reached. Even the "hard cases." Many of the priests committed their lives to Christ.

Personal presentation can add the next forty percent to the effectiveness of the church's evangelistic efforts. Why? It is because every church has an army of members who can reach every lost person through organized evangelistic visitation and their own personal witness in the marketplace. Every member has a circle of influence! If the membership of a church is trained and equipped to share Christ, they can reach their family, friends, and acquaintances. Their daily traffic pattern causes them to meet people every day who need Christ. Through being trained to share Jesus and lead people to Christ, they will have the opportunity to lead people to him every day. They will be sensitive to the people they meet and to the Holy Spirit. The result is they will lead many to Christ. They will be involved in public proclamation, caring ministry, event attraction, and geographic saturation. The synergism of the interaction of all of these techniques will result in a church being evangelistically effective.

Each of the five techniques alone will reach fewer people for Christ without the other four. But to effectively reach multitudes for Christ, all five are needed. This will give the synergism that contributes to the maximum effectiveness of the church in evangelistic outreach.

The challenge we face is to strategically use all five of these biblical techniques to cause our churches to be as effective as they can be in reaching the lost!